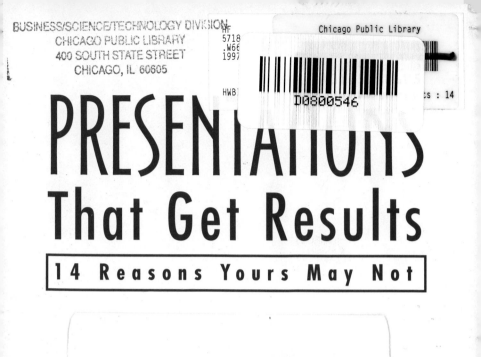

PRESENTATIONS
That Get Results

14 Reasons Yours May Not

PRESENTATIONS
That Get Results

14 Reasons Yours May Not

MARIAN K. WOODALL

PROFESSIONAL BUSINESS COMMUNICATIONS
Lake Oswego, OR 97035

Also by Marian K. Woodall:

Thinking On Your Feet – softcover
Thinking On Your Feet – audio cassette
Speaking To A Group – soft cover
How To Talk So Men Will Listen – soft cover
How To Talk So Men Will Listen – audio cassette
14 Reasons Corporate Speeches Don't Get the Job Done – soft cover

Printed and bound in the United States of America

Current printing
10 9 8 7 6 5 4 3 2 1

Library of Congress Cataloging-in-Publication Data
Woodall, Marian K., 1941–
   Presentations that get results : 14 reasons yours may not /
Marian K. Woodall.
     p. cm.
   Includes bibliographical references and index.
   ISBN 0-941159-97-3
   1. Business presentations.   2. Business communication.
I. Title.
HF5718.22.W66   1997
658.4'5–dc21   97-4729
                                CIP

Published by Professional Business Communications
15800 S.W. Boones Ferry Rd., Suite C-203
Lake Oswego, OR 97035-3456

DEDICATION

To my brothers Parker G and Bill —

good friends, great role models,
candid critics, strong supporters.

THE 14 REASONS:

REASON 1 – *"That's the way we've always done it."*

REASON 2 – *"It doesn't matter who's in the audience, this is our story."*

REASON 3 – *"What do you mean, 'What's our purpose?' "*

REASON 4 – *"I'm an expert. I just like to wing it."*

REASON 5 – *"We just read what the speechwriter gives us."*

REASON 6 – *"If I don't write it all out, I'll forget something."*

REASON 7 – *"My messsage usually covers about ten points"*

REASON 8 – *"We're selling a product. Of course we talk mostly about features."*

REASON 9 – *"We begin our presentations with our biography."*

REASON 10 – *"We repeat the points from our written proposal."*

REASON 11 – *"We don't need visuals."*

REASON 12 – *"You bet we have visuals...the fanciest visuals electronics can create."*

REASON 13 – *"I have enthusiasm. That's the key thing."*

or

"I'm too nervous to let my enthusiasm show."

REASON 14 – *"It's a speech, not a workshop. Why would I want to involve the audience?"*

TABLE OF CONTENTS

REASON 9

"We begin our presentations with our biography."

REASON 10

"We repeat the points from our written proposal."

REASON 11

"We don't need visuals."

REASON 12

"You bet we have visuals...the fanciest visuals electronics can create."

INTRODUCTION

If It Ain't Broke, Break It. That's the title of Robert Kriegel's book describing the need for constant change in corporate America. It's also the thesis for this book. Kriegel's contention is that through electronics and computers the world is moving so fast that corporations must keep reinventing themselves. Kriegel asserts that managers must constantly assess what they do, why they do it, whether it's effective. This continual assessment mandates change.

Reading his book, scenes from recent presentation coaching work with clients flashed upon my mental screen; I was stunned by the validity of Kriegel's message. Corporate messages have definitely not kept pace. Nowhere in the world of business have fewer changes been made. Products change, marketing materials change, software changes, but presentations have not changed.

Corporate messages are still in the 1970's. Old-fashioned "me-oriented" and "us-oriented" talks are lingering in the files and floating around the board room. Presidents and CEO's still read manuscripts describing the history of the company in boring detail. CFO's have access to exciting electronics packages which create state-of the-art graphics, yet they continue to flash up slides of deadly balance sheets crammed with numbers depicting last quarter's financial results. Marketing managers have exciting new promotional materials, yet in presentations they persist in relating feature by feature every nuance of each new product.

Presentations matter. Companies credit excellence in communicating as a key to their success. The ability to communicate ranks high in skills sought through the job interview. Promotion depends on the employee's ability to communicate. Everyone understands that a person's idea can be no stronger than his ability to get it across. Despite all this awareness, messages in business lag behind.

The material for this attack on the old way of preparing speeches and presentations comes primarily from experiences with my clients, in speech coaching, in training, and in assistance to speech writers. Thanks to each of you for being an example, whether good and awful. Since industry names were changed and there are no company names, no one will recognize you; when you recognize yourself, my congratulations that you're already changing!

Each of the fourteen reasons is written to stand alone, as a reference. The inevitable overlap exists. One way to emphasize the importance of an idea — in a book as well as in presentation or speech — is to repeat it. So I have.

Corporate presentations are broken, and they need to be fixed.

Find your weak spots and correct them. Make your corporate messages as fine as your product or service. You owe your company no less.

REASON 1

"That's the way we've always done it."

The Problem:
Corporate America is developing '90's corporate messages using '70's models.

The Solution:
Make your corporate message timely: make sure it's as new as your product or service. Bring your visual aids up to date with new technology.

What's Wrong With the Way You've Always Done It?

You know. How successful would your company be if your product hadn't changed in 20 years? Would you still be in business? Not likely. How many repeat customers would you have if your customer service practices hadn't kept pace with changing needs? Not many. Yet corporate message development and delivery haven't kept pace. Too often, a new manager comes in, looks at the files, examines how the last speaker handled this subject, substitutes new numbers and figures, and gives the same old presentation. Or a new speechwriter is hired, looks at the files, examines what's been done, and prepares the next speech for the president in the same old way.

Imagine what happens in a company when suggestions to upgrade product development or customer service are met with the objection, *But that's the way we've always done it.* Yet questions about speech approaches are often met with that response. Following Kriegel's idea, *we've always done it this way* is the number one reason to use fresh approaches. *We've always done it this way* is a problem not only because times have changed, but also because it's highly likely the way you did it wasn't so successful anyway. The impact of television and the advances in electronics and graphics make it even more vital to change the way things have always been done.

Your presentations need to be as good as your product or your service; it rarely happens. Poor corporate speeches make no sense. Companies spend bundles of money on professional product brochures and glossy annual reports, but let their executives represent those fancy brochures with black and white overheads created on their laser printer. Corporations spend thousands of dollars sending their staff to motivational workshops, and no dollars on presentation skills training. One giant high tech firm recently spent over $25,000 creating and producing a state-of-the-art book on new technology plus countless additional dollars sending a full-time trainer across the globe for two day sessions on the material — yet they wouldn't authorize an additional $2500 for fresh overheads using the graphics from the books.

Academic speeches are a prime example of the problem of reluctance to change. Professors report their research findings at conferences; 99% of the time they prepare a paper containing the results plus all the relevant statistics, and they read it. They continue reading papers even though most realize cold statistics are boring and listening to a paper being read is even more boring. Why do they continue with this tired approach? Because that's the way they've always done it. Wouldn't it be stimulating if the speech contained interesting stories and anecdotes about the topic and the research activities, leaving the stats and the results to be summarized on handouts?

Another example of this widespread problem is evident in safety training sessions. The unlucky soul drafted to present the training too often bad mouths her own presentation, running it and the entire topic down with a comment such as, I know this is boring but we've got to go through it. She then proceeds to read her speech on the regulations, enumerating each one by painful one because that's the way she's always done it.

Whether you are a manager creating your own speech, an assistant creating some notes for your boss's presentation, the corporate speechwriter, or the CEO, recognize the tired mental set which says *that's the way we've always done it,* decide to do whatever is in your power to make changes.

New Times Require New Approaches

Change is everywhere. Even if there had been no exciting new electronics, no rapid advance in graphics and the ability to create visuals that support messages, it would still be important to change messages. Products and services have changed. Organizations have changed. Messages have not changed. Most firms still employ a horse-and-buggy presentation style in a supersonic world.

How has your organization changed? Answer these questions:

- What's different about our product from the last time we presented to this audience?
- What's different about our services from the last time we presented this material?
- Are our goals different?
- Is our mission statement different?
- Do we have a new logo?
- Do we have new business cards?
- Do we have a new president?
- Do we have a new speech approach?

If your company's products are ready for the 90's but your presentations are still in the 70's, make some changes.

Take-away Sentence:

Make your presentations as superior as your product or service.

REASON 2

"It doesn't matter who's in the audience, this is our story."

The Problem:
It's not what you want to say that matters; it's what the audience wants to hear — or needs to hear, is ready for, or will sit still for — that matters.

The Solution:
The presentation is for the audience, not the speaker.

Why Is Talking Mostly About Yourself a Problem?

When you present the same corporate message, with the same details about the product or service no matter who's in the audience, you indulge the speaker, leaving the audience behind. Members of the audience want you to answer their question, *What's in it for me?* If the audience is potential buyers, they want to hear how the product will benefit them, not just what its features are. If a speech for the staff is about new goals in customer service or better selling methods, what the audience needs to hear is **how** they can make the change, not just company rhetoric about its im—

portance. If the material is new technical knowledge about an update in the company-wide computer system, the message must be what the audience is ready to understand, which may not be the technical level you're comfortable with. When presenting a proposal to the Board of Directors, the message must be the amount of information the audience will sit still for, not everything you'd like to say.

You give a speech for the audience, not for yourself. If you simply stand up and say what you want to say, it's cheaper just to talk into a mirror. Speakers can be classed by attitude into two categories: those who say, *Here I am,* and those who say, *There you are.* Be sure you're in the latter category.

The primary way to move people is see a topic from their perspective; walk over to where they're standing and say, *Yes. Now I see what it looks like from here.* Another way to become comfortable with the concept that the message is for the audience is to consider the presentation as a journey. You can be the driver and the tour guide, but the journey is for the passengers: the audience.

A Journey Focusing on the Audience

Here are four keys to unlocking that journey for both you and the audience:

- the **destination** = a **one-sentence take-away message** indicating where you want to take the audience.
- the **vehicle** = **your purpose,** the transportation to get them to the desired destination.
- the **map** = the **outline,** the route you travel, including names of the stops along the way.
- the **perspective setter** = the **hook** or opener, which establishes that it is their trip.

The Destination. The destination is where you want the message to wind up. It's the take-away sentence, the point you want the audience to remember. One idea is about all an audience can remember. So the best way to identify your destination is to develop it in a single sentence. If your audience is potential investors, your single sentence could be, *Consolidated's strategy is paying off.* If your purpose is to kindle a cooperative spirit within a diverse audience, the sentence can be, *The word for today is* **connecting**.

Here are examples of take-away messages for the audiences described above:

- potential buyers, *You can increase profits by selling these accessories as add-on's.*
- staff customer service goals, *You'll go home happier if your customers go home happier.*
- staff computer update, *Take a day to learn it, then save half a day a week using it.*
- the proposal to your board, *Productivity can be increased up to 30% with the purchase of the automated system.*

Too often, presentations are not successful because the speaker doesn't have a specific idea about outcome — the destination. If you can state that destination in one sentence, you have that outcome clearly in mind. This degree of focus is necessary because you can get them to only one place. Though there may be intermediate stops along the way, a trip can have only one destination.

The Vehicle. The **purpose** of the presentation is the transportation for the trip. Decisions about purpose and take away message often come hand in hand. Without knowing the destination, it's difficult to know precisely what the vehicle should be. Too often clients greet my question, *What's the purpose of this presentation?* with a long silence. When you have the take-away message established, it's easy to decide on the purpose, although sometimes awareness of purpose comes first. Purpose generally fits into one of four basic categories:

- inform
- educate
- persuade, convince, or build goodwill
- get action.

What you need to get done is the purpose. In a presentation of an hour or less, you can get only one thing done well. Only one of these four can be the primary purpose. Understand the situation and know the audience to determine which of these is your real goal, your purpose. That purpose becomes your vehicle, the transportation by which you are going to move the audience to its destination.

Getting people to **yes** is a process; taken together, these four purposes are the steps in that process. For a presentation to be successful you need to start at the appropriate step for that particular audience. See Reason Three for more on that process and on defining your purpose.

The Map. The outline is the map, the route that you will take, including the stops you plan along the way. You can think of it as a frame which holds up your presentation, or a superstructure that you impose upon the material.

You need focus. A trip with many stops and just a few minutes at each, is not a memorable trip. *If this is Tuesday, it must be Belgium* isn't a very good way to see Europe. Presentations are the same. If you make many points, (as discussed in Reason Seven), the au–

dience will not come away with your message. Plan only two or three stops along the route; make only two or three main points, spending a good amount of time at each one. Make each point memorable, with stories, illustrations, vivid graphics, or found objects that highlight and reinforce those points; your audience will have a strong, specific memory of your material. They will remember the trip.

A test for success in a presentation is this: Someone who was not at your speech can call someone who was there and find out what your message was. It should go something like this:

> Fred: *What did John from XYZ Corporation have to say about the new benefits package?*
> Nancy: *It will take a little while to get used to the changes, but we'll save more money.*
> Fred: *That's it?*
> Nancy: *That's it. It will take a little while to get used to it, but it will save money.*

Make sure your presentations can pass that test.

The Hook. The opener, the first sentence out of your mouth, is the hook that captures the attention of the audience. No one is thinking about the topic except you. A good hook connects with those minds thinking about something else, gathering their attention to your topic. A hook may be a statistic, a comparison, a quotation, a challenge, a question, or your strongly worded one-sentence message. A great hook is a memorable one-liner, what the media calls a soundbite.

The hook talks about the audience to the audience. The hook sets their perspective. It lets them know the trip is theirs. Use **You.** Say, *You will find...*, *You will save* *money...*, an immediate signal that the speech is for the audience; the focus will be on their needs and wants, rather than on your information and features. Avoid using *I* or *we*, especially early in the presentation. These two pronouns signal that it's going to be **your** trip. Avoid hooks such as, *I would like to tell you about...*, *We are very proud of...*, which signal the wrong perspective. (See Reason Nine for more tips on openers.)

Technical Expertise
Not What the Audience Needs to Hear

Jargon signals that your speech is what you want to say rather than what the audience needs to hear. Technical terms and jargon are part of your arena, but not necessarily part of theirs. It is natural to employ words that you use everyday; however, in most speaking situations your level of expertise is higher than that of the audience. Think in the vocabulary of your profession if you need to as you plan, but translate that technical jargon into non-technical language for the speech.

Financial data is one professional area in which jargon is a major obstacle. Accounting, financial analysis and financial planning professionals are comfortable with the verbal tools of their trade; most of their audiences are very uncomfortable with this language. A funds management client took exception to that observation when assessing his firm's typical audiences: committees and boards who had oversight for their company's pension funds. He protested, *Oh, but this committee makes the decisions about their funds; they know the language just as well as we do.* My response, *Wrong. For you it's a full time job; for the committee members it's something they do beyond their regular job of plant manager, union shop steward, or middle manager.* Even the VP of finance doesn't spend all day every day using the jargon of the Stock Market.

When the technical expertise among members of your audience varies, as is frequently the case, one of two decisions guides your choice of language: what's the differential between how much I know and how much most of them know? or what's the level of technical comfort of the decision maker? Any time you're in doubt, choose simpler vocabulary. Your goal is to speak so that you cannot be misunderstood. It's rare that you would speak too simply or too clearly.

Take-away Sentence:

Say what the audience needs to hear,
not what you want to say.

REASON 3

"What do you mean, 'What's our purpose?'"

The Problem:
  Two basic problems exist when considering the purpose of a presentation:
  - no purpose
  - too many purposes.

  Both problems create equally unsuccessful speeches. How can a speech be successful if you aren't certain what you want it to accomplish? or if it has so many purposes the audience can't sort them out?

The Solution:
  Know why you're giving a speech. Decide what part of the larger message will be appropriate for this audience at this time.

Why Is Lack of Clear Purpose a Problem?

Someone asks you the purpose of your speech. If you respond, *What do you mean, "what's our purpose?" We're going to the conference to talk about our new product,* you are approaching the speech — and the conference — from the wrong direction.

A response which indicates that you understand your purpose is, *Our purpose is to **educate** the conference attendees about the benefit of our new product.*

If you respond, *What do you mean "What's our purpose?" We're on the short list for that contract. We're going to tell them what our background is,* you're approaching the oral portion of a proposal with the wrong purpose. An appropriate response is, *Our purpose is to convince the prospect that their team and our team have a great fit, so they'll choose us for the job.*

Whether presenting at a conference, appearing in front of prospective buyers or clients, making a pitch to a professional organization, or describing the company and its products, there must be a specific purpose. Going to talk about your product or yourself is not that purpose, because that's what you want to say, not what the audience wants or needs to hear.

An alternate response I often hear is, *We're going to introduce our new product, describe its outstanding features and explain how they work. Then we'll be taking orders for it.* That approach will be equally unsuccessful, because it has too many purposes; people don't move that fast.

A speech needs a purpose — but only one. A strong positive statement in answer to the question, *what's your purpose?* reaffirms your specific purpose for the speech. You know what the purpose is. You have a sense of the situation and the audience, and your speech gets the job done by making sure that the speech is appropriate. Remember the speech as a journey: the **purpose** is the vehicle, the transportation you use to get the audience to the desired destination.

A Speech Is Only Part of a Process

Clients say the difficulty with narrowing down to a single purpose is that there is much they want to accomplish. Of course. The ultimate goal of nearly all speeches is to get a *yes*. The bottom line is that last category of purpose, to get action. The ultimate prize is get the sale, get the contract signed, retain them as clients, call our customer service number if they are not happy. Getting to **yes** is a process, and all four primary purposes — inform, educate, convince, get action — are steps in that process.

Your difficulties occur when you think your purpose is "get action," but the audience isn't ready for that step. See the larger picture. Look at the four steps in the whole process: inform, educate, convince, get action. Give yourself permission to do only the doable in any one presentation. To understand what is doable, consider two guides for presenting:

- Your particular presentation is one piece of a larger process;
- Your particular presentation is not the whole story (see Reason Seven).

A Speech as Part of a Process. Consider the first concept — your presentation is part of a large process — in the context of financial planning. Selecting the services of a financial planner can be a long and complex procedure. People first have to be aware that financial planning exists. Next, they have to be educated about how financial planning works, how planners work, and why they can retire more comfortably if they use some financial planning. Third, they must be convinced of four separate points: financial planning is appropriate for them; they don't have enough knowledge to do the planning themselves; they should utilize the services of a professional, someone knowledgeable, trained, and experienced; you are the specific professional they should work with. The fourth step in the procedure is taking the action, making an appointment and setting up the actual financial plans.

See the multiple purposes at work here? Information, education, convincing, convincing, convincing, convincing, and action. This one scenario uses all four basic categories of purpose. See why you can't do it all in one speech?

Perhaps your audience is a group of people who know financial planning exists but don't know much about it. To find out what part of the process this audience needs to hear, your decision should be *Through **education**, my goal is to help this audience understand why financial planning would be helpful for them.*

Or this may be your situation: This audience is a frustrated stocks and bonds club. They are knowledgeable about financial planning. This audience is in a different part of the process; they are prospective clients. *Through **persuasion**, I hope to get some of them as clients for me.*

Find out where the intended audience is in the procedure and making your only-one-purpose decision will be easy.

Discovering Where in the Process Your Audience Is

Once again, the four basic categories of purpose are

- inform
- educate
- convince, persuade, or build goodwill
- get action.

While more than one of these purposes may be part of the material of the presentation, only one major purpose must be clearly identified in your mind as the primary purpose.

Inform. To inform is to pass along information, statistics, data, or opinions to a group of people. That's the most difficult kind of speech to give because the potential for boredom is high (for both the audience and the speaker). If you are certain that all you're going to do is inform, send a memo or a letter, or write a short report. It's difficult to stay interesting as a speaker, and it's equally difficult to stay interested as an audience when the purpose is just to inform.

Educate. To educate is to provide information with the specific goal that the audience will use the information at some point. Unlike informing, educating implies a future use for the knowledge. And, unlike training, the knowledge won't be applied immediately. Educating an audience is generally less detailed and more theoretical than training or instructing them. Your assessment of the audience helps to determine the level of language and the organizational approach that will be helpful.

Convince or Build Good Will. Convincing an audience requires that you move their minds. Though sometimes based on similar information as educating, convincing both presents and uses the knowledge differently. Your own feelings are strong in a speech to persuade. This purpose is identified by the nature of language that you use, the kind of spin you put on phrases or concepts, the emotional appeal of stories that you select. Your goal is to alter the minds of the audience by what you say.

Get Action. If your primary purpose is to get action, you say, especially at the end, **exactly** what you want them to do:

Send your check today.
Sign up for this wonderful seminar.
Write your congressional representative.
Write a letter to the newspaper.
Resolve to change your life.

Action is the ultimate goal, but it's one you can success-fully reach only after the other three steps have been ac-complished. Too often, a speaker, especially a speaker who is trying to sell services or get donations, will include all four steps as purposes, trying to do the whole thing. You have been asked by a friend to join her in hearing about a new charitable cause. You have never heard of it and don't know a thing about it. But it would be good to see your friend, and it seems like a nice thing to do, so you go. For an hour, you sit in a cold church basement or an over-heated restaurant, listening to an impassioned speaker who tries to (1) inform you that the problem exists, (2) educate you about the scope and seriousness of the prob-lem, (3) convince you that it is a problem of such magni-tude and importance that you will consider supporting it, and (4) get you to write a check that very night. It just doesn't happen. We just don't move that fast, especially where parting with some of our money is the main focus.

So while getting action is the ultimate goal, your pur-pose must be tailored to which step in the larger process your audience is ready for.

Assessing the Audience

Use this assessment tool, the Communications Triangle, to find out where your audience is in the larger process.

As you assess the communications triangle, ask yourself these questions:

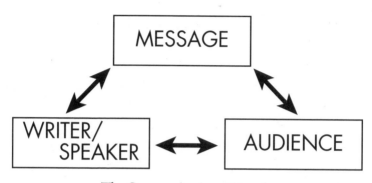

The Communications Triangle
©1979, Marian K. Woodall

- Who is the audience?
- Who am I in relation to this audience?
- What is the general message that needs to be communicated to this audience?
- What is my relationship to the message?
- What is the audience's relationship to the message?
- How do all these aspects relate, and what do these relationships tell me about the way I should approach my material?

Sometimes the makeup of the audience is difficult to assess. Make the best assessment you can — on the basis of their age, their education, the kind of organization they are a part of and so on. Based on your assessment, judge which step most of them are at in the process: they need information, or education, to be convinced or are ready to sign up. Decide your purpose and pitch your message there.

It's hard to stop short of asking for action. How can you justify stopping short of asking for the job? Consider the financial planners example again. Recognize there are other people in the process. Articles in newspapers, business magazines, even popular magazines, have **informed** people about the importance of financial planning especially for retirement.

Depending on their sophistication, someone may already have **educated** them to the possibility of better retirement by using professional financial planners. So, you **should** convince them they need to do it sooner rather than later. Suddenly you realize **convincing** is your purpose, and here's your one sentence: *The sooner you plan your financial future the better that future will be.*

You reason, *Oh, but if I can convince them, then why can't I also get them to sign up?* A few in the audience may, those who move rapidly. They were already further along in the process. Some will come up afterwards and ask for your card. But they're the exception rather than the rule.

You protest, *Yes, but, I want to get their business. Can't I convince them that it's important and get them to call me at the same time?* Probably not. But have a drawing, get their cards, and do a follow-up phone call or mailing. Your brochures at the back of the room perform another part of the process.

Have a doable purpose. Your particular presentation can accomplish only one step of the process; find that appropriate step for an audience and you can get them to the destination you have chosen. Someone else — probably you — will do the next steps in the process through other means: follow-up calls, letters, brochures, advertising.

(The second speaking guide, that no speech is the whole story, can be found in Reason Seven.)

Take-away Sentence:

Know your precise purpose
and be sure it's doable.

REASON 4

"I'm an expert. I just like to wing it."

The Problem:
Experts think that it's OK to wing it because they have so much knowledge. Yet they are often the least successful speakers, precisely because of their knowledge. Experts generally overwhelm an audience rather than enlighten it.

The Solution:
Organize your knowledge and then provide a structure for it. A speech is like a data base: you've got to organize it. Without structure, client information is not a data base; it's just data, and it's not very useful. The more knowledge you possess, the greater the need for structure to organize it. Knowledge won't be useful to the audience unless is has some structure.

What's the Matter With Winging It?

Winging it means not preparing. One of the most famous nineteenth century orators Daniel Webster said, *I'd rather be half naked than half prepared* for a speaking engagement. The problem with lack of preparation it not having a focus for the presentation. Without focus, lots of information does not accomplish anything specific. Wingers don't determine the primary purpose of the speech ahead of time. Wingers don't develop a one sentence message ahead of time. Because wingers don't know where they want to take the audience, they don't take them anywhere. If you don't have a destination, you'll never know if you've arrived.

Paradoxically, then, the more you know about a topic, the more important it is for you to be organized. Provide a structure to narrow and focus your knowledge. Plan a take-away sentence. Plan the purpose.

Three common scenarios create problems for the expert:

- tangents
- content with no structure
- great delivery with no message.

Tangents. Experts are interesting, even compelling, to listen to. But the goal of corporate messages is seldom *Be interesting.* For a corporate message to get the job done, it needs to accomplish a specific purpose.

Even if an expert knows where she wants to take an audience, she often goes off on tangents. One type of tangent is telling wonderful, enthusiastic stories. These stories, however entertaining, generally don't get the audience to a desired destination because they aren't supporting anything.

Another tangent trap for experts is getting mired down in minute details. These details may be fascinating, but they obscure the message. The expert gets side-tracked, running out of time before he reaches his goal.

Another variation on the tangent is the expert who drowns the audience in information. Telling examples of this expert problem are former NBA coaches who provide color analysis for televised professional basketball games. Mike Fratello, Doug Collins, and Hubie Brown are three such coaches whose knowledge is encyclopedic; unfortunately they tell their viewers much more than is appropriate at a given moment. Their words overwhelm the play they're describing.

Much Content, No Structure. Some categories of speakers worry about having enough to say; the problem with executives is that they have too much to say. Content itself is not the problem; having too much content is the problem. Vast quantities of information increase the need to be selective. With so much knowledge, it's easy to say to yourself, *I've got so much work to do this week. I know this material. I'll just go talk to them for awhile. It'll be fine.* It won't be fine. You may be comfortable, even relaxed. Your audience may be relaxed. But chances are you won't accomplish anything specific because you didn't have anything specific planned. You won't take them anywhere because you hadn't planned a destination.

Good Speaker, No Message. Everyone has had the experience of hearing a good speaker with no message. As you leave the auditorium, you overhear someone say, *Wow, wasn't that wonderful? She's so good. What a dynamic speaker. That was really —* And then they pause, because upon examination, it wasn't anything. When asked what the speaker had to say, their response is apt to be,

> *I don't know. It was very good. She's a good speaker.*
> *But what did she say?*
> *Well, she talked about retirement.*
> *What did she say about retirement?*
> *I really can't tell you.*

The good speaker needs structure even more than the beginning or intermediate speaker. Do not wing it. Have a structure.

Create Structure That Includes Oral Guidelines

The best structure helps in two ways: you use it to plan your presentation and your audience uses it to follow your speech. I call such a structure **Oral Guidelines.** Oral guidelines help burn your message into the minds of the audience. Consider this help:

- They force you to be organized.
- They divide and frame the content.
- Naming and numbering helps the audience follow your material.
- They are your means of reclaiming listeners when their minds drift away.

Forcing You To Be Organized. You select, from all you know about the subject, the 2% that's relevant for this particular audience. You organize that 2% logically. You decide on the take-away sentence and the purpose. The oral guidelines provide the physical organization by naming and numbering your main sections. (See Reason Seven for the Two Percent Rule.)

Dividing and Framing Your Content. Think of oral guidelines as headings and subheadings. Your material is broken into smaller units of information, making it easier to absorb in exactly the same way headings and subheadings break up a written report. These oral guidelines divide the material into sections and frame each section. Each section should have its own one-sentence message, its own opener and conclusion. Because each section has a distinct message, it can stand alone. In case time is short and you must eliminate some content, an entire section, heading and all, can easily be eliminated. Here is an example of oral guidelines as part of the text of your speech:

> *Increase your profits by adding accessories to your lines of merchandise.* [the hook]
> *Accessories enable you to provide **three** aspects of added value to your customers: essential accessories, related products, one-stop shopping.* [the rest of the introduction]

First, consider the need your customers have for accessories, including batteries, extension cords....

The **second** value added aspect you can offer is related products....

Finally, give your customers the opportunity of one-stop shopping....

Naming and Numbering. Oral guidelines enable the audience to anticipate what you are going to say. They are the road map for the journey. Because each of these individual sections can be named and numbered, they provide the framework that supports the presentation; the numbering divides the material logically no matter which organizational pattern you choose. This structure also helps the audience to "see" the speech as you give it.

Reclaiming the Audience. Finally the guidelines provide a mechanism to regather the attention of listeners whose minds have drifted away. Being able to get the audience listening again is essential, because people can listen intently for just a short while. If the speaker is extremely compelling, they may listen for a few minutes. No one listens intently for even ten minutes, let alone an hour.

To see all these purposes for oral guidelines at work, consider the sermon. People who address congregations are trained (or seem to be) to use oral guidelines. Listen to the minister who begins his sermon by saying, *The text for today is sin. There are three kinds of sin to examine this morning: your sin, my sin, and our sin.* The minister has named and numbered the guidelines. The audience knows that there will be three different topics, three divisions to the sermon. They are prepared to hear and absorb three points.

The minister gets into the body of the sermon by individually naming and numbering his first major point: *The first kind of sin for our attention this morning is your sin.* He makes comments, tells the relevant stories. During the time that he's speaking the support material, the audience tends to mentally drift away. People woolgather. They notice the beautiful light coming in through the stained glass. They look at the wonderful flowers at the altar.

How does the minister get his listeners back? The skillful minister knows about wool gathering; when he comes to the second main point, he not only repeats the oral guideline, he also repeats the number: *The second kind of sin is my sin.* The minister develops this second point, the audience again mentally drifts away. Once again recaptures listeners with the oral guidelines.

And finally, ladies and gentlemen, we are forced to consider our sins. For the third section of the sermon, he again gets them listening.

You see by this example that the oral guidelines actually tell the audience how many main points there are, signalling each main point as it occurs. People will listen as long as they need to, to get the point, to understand the concept; then their minds will drift away. Oral guidelines reclaim them as listeners.

The same speech can be given, with exactly the same words and the same support and examples, but without the structure of oral guidelines; it's one uninterrupted long speech. Listening to an unstructured speech is like reading a multi-page report with no headings or subheads — difficult. The oral guidelines interrupt a long speech, turning it into several shorter, more graspable divisions, each of which can be absorbed individually. Don't miss the chance to help your audience help you to succeed. Provide the listening structure of oral guidelines.

Take-away Sentence:

The greater your knowledge,
the more you need structure.

REASON 5

"We just read what the speechwriter gives us."

The Problem:
Thinking someone else can fully prepare **your** speech.

The Solution:
Work with your speechwriter: help to describe the audience, discuss the purpose, provide the take-away sentence, offer some stories or anecdotes.

Why Can't the Speechwriter Prepare Your Speech?

A busy executive will ask the speechwriter to prepare a speech for an upcoming occasion. She glances over it briefly on the way to the conference, and then reads the speech. Absolutely unsuccessful. Here are three main reasons that speeches written by speechwriters and read by speakers do not get the job done:

- It's generally not your message; it's someone else's idea of the message;
- You can't say it like you mean it, because you don't mean it;
- Reading won't do it. You have to rehearse.

It's Not Your Message

It's difficult to be enthusiastic about someone else's message. But that's the speech you get, unless you are prepared, organized, and know how to work with your speechwriter.

What do you usually do? Give him the name of the conference and some information about the proposed topic. The speechwriter will struggle, because he needs more information. But because he's subordinate to you in the organization, he is hesitant to insist. And if he does ask, chances are you wouldn't know what he needs either or you'd already have told him. He sits down at the computer and writes something. But you won't be able to deliver it successfully.

Here's what happens. I was asked to help the vice president of marketing for a major software company in the Northwest who was notorious for being unwilling to give presentations. In fact, he'd never been on a press tour. His firm decided that he absolutely must do the press tour for a particularly important new release in his division.

The speechwriter wrote a speech. The VP said to his handlers, *I can't say this.* I was called to see if I could help out, and a copy of the speech was faxed to me. It was a beautiful speech to read. It included long, resonant passages which developed a lovely theme looking at the past and the future of communications in wonderfully appealing ways. The theme was developed with a tremendous extended metaphor about buffaloes racing across the prairie, their thundering hooves echoing in the distance.

It was well written, and it read beautifully. But it was not written to be delivered. It was written like a magazine article.

I suspected that the speechwriter hadn't ever given a speech. He had also not read any of this speech out loud, to test whether it was deliverable. The result was obvious: As a speech it was dreadful.

The nervous, angry vice president came in, flung his copy across the table towards me, and said, *I can't give this stuff.* And he was right: It was not even close to being his message.

I grabbed the copy, dramatically ripping it apart, and flung it into the wastebasket. *You're exactly right, you can't. Let's create something quickly that you can say.* When I inquired about what he wanted to say about the software, out came a coherent single sentence. I said, *That's it. That's the message. What are two or three reasons why that's true?*

What do you mean? he responded.

*Well, **why** do you believe that?"*

Oh, yeah. He quickly wrote down a couple of ideas. For his fifteen minute presentation, two points were enough. When asked if he had any stories, illustrations, anecdotes, to support these two points he laughed, *Oh, yeah,* and easily related a longish client story, which was humorous, entertaining, and revealing.

He jotted down a note or two about the story, and I said, *There's your speech. You can say it as if you mean it, because you do mean it. Here's your one-sentence message, two supporting points, and a story to illustrate them. That's all you have to do.*

He replied, *That's all? I don't have to talk about the buffaloes thundering across the prairie? That's a relief!*

The story has a happy ending. With his own message, he went to the press conference, confidently delivered his one sentence, added two points, and told his story. All the while he managed to relax and smile. He was pleased with his first attempt at a public presentation.

You Have to Mean It

Nothing is harder to fake than enthusiasm. Delivering a manuscript, you especially need words you can say as if you mean them. You can't create interest among the audience when you don't have any yourself. It's easy for speakers to say, as my clients do, *Well, I'm not really very excited about this. It's just part of my job.* Of course it's just part of your job. You're a professional. Speaking is part of what you do, so learn to do it well and learn to make it interesting.

And you can make it interesting. I often ask a client to bring a found object, an item from the office, something that reminds him of something he likes a great deal. It's usually a photograph, a baby shoe, or a trophy. I ask them to stand up and talk about the item. Because the item is important, most people can talk about it easily. They have natural enthusiasm. Laughter and smiles are common. When they see a videotape of this relaxed performance, clients understand they do have the ability to be enthusiastic and real. They soon realize it is possible to develop a similar level of enthusiasm in their professional presentations.

Bill Clinton is a current example of someone using a manuscript who delivers the speech as if he means it. He generates enthusiasm which reaches his audience. He uses speechwriters. He tells them a great deal about what he wants. He has them start each speech early so there is time for many drafts and iterations. He edits their drafts, tweaking the message, all the way through the process. They write; he makes notes, adds and subtracts things; it goes back and forth again, again, again. — even up to the point of his delivery.

When President Clinton presented his economic message to the joint houses of Congress in February 1993 he made changes even after the speech had been computerized for the teleprompter. The teleprompter operator had to make allowances for the adjustments Clinton made right at the lectern as he was delivering.

Even though Clinton was reading from a clear plexiglass teleprompter, real force and enthusiasm were reflected in his voice. His audience could tell he meant it. He got these kinds of words by helping his speechwriter create a message he meant.

Help Yourself By Helping Your Speechwriter. Writing a speech for another is not easy. It should be a collaborative effort. The speaker needs to be intimately involved in the speechwriter's process. Make your wishes known. If the words of the speech sound like you want them to sound, you'll be able to mean them.

Why help your speechwriter? Recognize that it is your speech, whoever creates it. You are the one whose reputation and credibility are on the line when you stand up in front of a group. Speechwriters say their executives resist taking time out to give assistance. Sometimes that's because executives don't put enough weight on the power of speaking. They often consider it an imposition to have to talk to the speechwriter, prepare some notes, or an outline to provide direction. The attitude too often is, *Well, that's what the speechwriter's for.* Wrong.

The job of speechwriter is to support you; if you don't want to help yourself, you deserve whatever kind of gobbledygook you get. When you help the speechwriter, the one you are helping is yourself.

How Can You Help the Speechwriter? Communicate with your speechwriter. Be sure she has opportunities to hear you speak, to hear your language and delivery, to observe your style and approach to an audience. Give her information about the speaking situation and the audience, and listen to her information about it.

Invite the speechwriter in for a discussion of the speech. Develop the focus together, by deciding the take-away sentence. This one sentence alone will improve the speechwriter's chance of giving you what you want. Decide on the purpose of the speech; define the main points to support the message. Discuss what this audience needs or wants to support that message.

If you have stories, examples, and illustrations, jot them down. The speechwriter doesn't know what kind of stories and experience you have, what anecdotes might be interesting and helpful. You are the one who knows.

You want a speech that you mean. Get it by helping the speechwriter.

Reading Won't Do It

A manuscript can be delivered well, but reading it isn't delivering it. If you just read, you'll be boring. Your voice won't be personable. Your inflections will be phony. Your pauses will be unnatural. Delivering from a manuscript is a skill which takes practice to develop, just as any skill takes practice.

Consider the anchor people on television, the professional news deliverers — the Diane Sawyers and the Tom Brokaws. They have learned to deliver from a script, via the teleprompter, so it sounds as if they are talking to the audience. Even though your style as a corporate speaker needs to be more personal, talking to the audience is your goal with a manuscript.

Enthusiasm is one key. One speechwriter put it this way, *When you speak to an audience you become a storyteller — a person who has something he or she is itching to share with someone — and it shows.* What if you aren't itching to share this particular message? It happens. Clients say, *Well, I just don't feel all that strongly about the topic.* Tough. You have two choices. Don't accept speaking opportunities you don't like, or else figure out ways to demonstrate that you do feel strongly about it. That's what being a representative of your product or company involves.

Describe Your Style. One key to helping get a manuscript that fits is to tell your writer about the particular styles of language you like. If you are an experienced speaker and you know your favorite rhetorical devices, tell the speechwriter so she can develop the right structures. For example:

- the rule-of-three: Lincoln's "...of the people, by the people, for the people"; Daniel Webster's "Liberty and union, now and forever, one and inseparable"; Danton's "...to dare, to dare again, ever to dare."
- the concept of balance, two phrases or sentences which have opposing elements such as Senator Barry Goldwater's famous quote, *Extremism in the defense of liberty is no vice, moderation in the pursuit of justice is no virtue.*
- alliteration. Remember former Vice President Spiro Agnew's *nattering nabobs of negativism.* This phrase struck a resonant chord, especially with newspaper people, because of the obscurity of the words and the strong sound of the alliteration.

- rhetorical questions, those used for effect, not to solicit a response in the audience. A rhetorical question is often a great opener for a speech: *Why, indeed, should we take more of our tax money to pay for yet another program?*
- hyperbole, exaggeration to emphasize a point, not to prove one. The financial vice president says, *Our stock is going down like Niagara Falls.* A speaker trying to convince an audience not to give in to negativism may, using hyperbole, say, *One-fifth of the people are against everything all the time.*

Short sentences sound more like people talk, longer sentences create a more formal tone. If you like a hard hitting presentation, you want short sentences that can be delivered with punch. If you like a more discursive style, request longer sentences with pauses and asides. Be sure that you can deliver those longer sentences with the appropriate pauses, so the idea still hangs together for the audience.

For a more casual speech, you want a more breezy style. Use contractions, perhaps even some slang, so long as the audience won't misunderstand, and jargon, provided the audience is apt to understand most of it. A breezy style can also make a serious speech sound less grave. But use this style carefully, so you aren't talking down to the audience; a breezy style can be misinterpreted as being condescending.

Tell the speechwriter also what you don't like. With specific suggestions about your style, she can create your tone.

Housekeeping Words to Avoid. Weed out the housekeeping phrases in your manuscript, or train your speechwriter not to use them. These phrases include what you are going to do, as opposed to your simply doing it.

For instance, *First, I'm going to talk about... Next, we'll discuss... Finally, let me give you an example of...* are housekeeping phrases which just talk about doing something. Consider the difference between

> *I want to tell you about the most significant change in the computer industry this year. That change is interactive computing.*

and

> *Interactive computing is the most significant change in the computer industry this year.*

The subject is the most important word in the sentence. When the subject of the sentence is one of these pronouns *I, me, my,* you put the emphasis on yourself as speaker rather than on the topic. You send the wrong message to the audience. Making the subject *interactive computing* sends the right message.

Speakers mistakenly use housekeeping phrases as part of transitions. The traditional but inappropriate transition — including the housekeeping phrase — is: *let me tell you about our plans for the future.* Cut that to *What about our plans for the future?* or, *Now, about our plans for the future.* or, *Finally, the plans for the future.* Transitions are important. Like subheadings in a report, these phrases signal what's next; housekeeping words are not needed.

In fact, in the ideal speech the words *I* or *we* do not appear. Focus all of your attention on the audience and what it needs or wants. Though difficult to accomplish, this ideal speech keeps you focused.

Exceptions to the ideal are few, but one is a personal experience. Drawing the audience to you with a personal example, you do need to use *I*.

Other ways to make a manuscript interesting is with concreteness. Add specific details. Or write shorter sentences. Remember that the ear is smaller than the mouth. Make the sentences short enough that the audience can grasp them. Sound interesting by using vivid language, words that appeal to all the senses so the audience can see, smell, taste and feel what you're talking about. Ask for words that create specific images. Instead of *Our goal is to talk about the budget,* try, *We expect to carve into our three million dollar budget.* Talk about *trees growing thick as the grass in lawns,* rather than *a dense forest.*

Manuscript Formatting for Delivery Success

In all speech giving, eye contact is essential. In manuscript delivery, it's harder to achieve than when speaking from notes or an outline. If a manuscript is written out in longhand or if handwritten changes are made at the last minute, legibility will create more problems. (See below for more on eye contact.) Small type, poor spacing, no colored annotations to indicate emphasis and pauses — all can cause you to fail.

Effective Formatting
- Use large type, something bigger than 12 point.
- Use caps and lower case, because you pick up the words by scanning the ascenders and descenders (the tops of *h* and *l* above the line, the tails of *p* and *y* below the line).
- Use bullets, indents, items in a series. A single glance will show the rhetorical structure of the words you'll be saying.
- Use at least double-spacing, with triple space between paragraphs, as a reminder to pause longer.

- Start new sections on new pages (or quadruple space before them.) to remind yourself to be firmer and more emphatic at the beginning of a new section.
- Don't split words by hyphenating at the end of a line.
- Use only the top two-thirds of the page to avoid the appearance of looking down at your belt.
- Number the pages at the top right corner so you see them quickly if you need to.
- End every page with a complete sentence, and a complete paragraph if possible.

I'll never forget hearing a CEO reading his manuscript say, near the close of a pre-holiday speech,

And to close, I would like to wish you all a very Merry
[Pause]
Christmas and a Happy New Year.

Rehearse, Rehearse, Rehearse

Another problem with just reading a manuscript prepared for you is that it's too easy to skip rehearsal. While you don't want to memorize it, you must learn it. Without rehearsal it's nearly impossible to learn it well enough to deliver it. The minimum rehearsal is reading it aloud, several times. Your four goals are

- hear the cadence
- check the flow
- be certain the words say what you want
- be sure you can move each sentence through your mouth and out to the audience without having unusual breaks.

Read a manuscript aloud at least three times to get it ready to rehearse. First reading is simply to see if it is deliverable (and to watch out for buffaloes thundering across the prairie). The second time through you begin to convey meaning, by including emphasis and pauses. Say each sentence, playing with emphasis and pauses. Begin marking it up with colored felt tip pens. But don't clutter it up. Don't get so involved in color-coding that you will become sidetracked by the codes.

To improve emphasis, mark these words:

- words that tell *who, what, when, where* and *why: One day* with *life* and *heart* is *more* than *time enough* to *find* a *world.* (Robert Lowell)
- nouns: The *president* gave his *oath* that the *country* would be served.
- verbs: Everyone *understood* the message; everyone *feared* the results.
- adjectives: The *private* conversations of *public* people are never *secret* conversations.

The third reading is for phrasing. A well-written speech is like a piece of music. It has a rhythm, which the speaker and the audience must feel. It has dynamic range. A good speaker learns to vary the tempo, slowing down, speeding up, whispering, speaking loudly.

I once worked on delivery with a reclusive CEO who hates speaking in public. His previous negative experience with speech coaches caused him to be less than enthusiastic about our work. The phrasing didn't seem to be popping out at him. On a hunch, I said, *This phrasing is just like the phrasing you learn when you play a musical instrument…. What do you play?*

Oh, he responded with a shy smile, *the violin.* [pause]

Ah, I see. Yes, let's try it again.

Luckily, I won his confidence and he won the phrasing contest. When you understand the phrasing, consider having the pages reformatted to reflect your phrasing marks. Each long phrase has its own line. Your eyes grasp the entire phrase with the briefest glance, you look at the audience, utter the entire phrase and pause at the end of it. Such formatting uses a few more pages, but improved eye contact and intonation make the extra pages well worth it.

Timing is another important aspect of your delivery. With a manuscript, as we have discussed, shorter sentences are better. For asides or parenthetical expressions, change the tone slightly, and pause, both before and after. To realize the impact, remember the master of timing, Jack Benny. He milked almost every pause for additional effect — and laughs.

Rehearse the entire presentation aloud several times in final, final format.

Tips on Manuscript Delivery Style. Eye contact matters. The rule of thumb is **no eye contact, no voice.** Be one-hundred percent eyes-up (looking at someone in the audience,) for your opener, all the oral guideline sentences and the closing sentence. To achieve such a high level of eye contact, these key sentences have to be memorized.

Aim for ninety percent eyes-up contact throughout. Though difficult to accomplish when delivering a manuscript, with sufficient practice and clear formatting it can be done. You have an idea of how much practicing you need to do.

The key to reaching ninety percent eye contact is to learn to look down in silence to find the next chunk. Don't begin speaking until you look up. The audience will wait for you;

they are absorbing what you just said. They don't expect you to be speaking every second. Here are the steps: Look down silently, absorb a chunk of material, and then look up, saying that chunk while you are looking at someone in the audience. Look down, absorb another chunk silently, look up, say that chunk. A major problem for people who use either manuscripts or extensive notes is a habit of looking down **in anticipation of the next sentence** before finishing the end of one they're saying. The end of each sentence is swallowed as they glance down for the next sentence. The result is loss of eye contact, voice emphasis, and voice projection.

Pauses. A master of the pause, Mark Twain, put it completely: *The pause is an exceedingly important feature in any kind of story.... It is a dainty thing and delicate, and also treacherous and uncertain, for it must be exactly the right length — no more no less — or else it fails its purpose and makes trouble.* So think of them as punctuation: a short pause for a comma; longer pause for a semicolon, colon, dots, or dashes; a definite pause for a period.

Pauses are silence, like white space in display advertisements or brochures. The silence between words is just as important as the words themselves; use silence to let a point sink in or allow a laugh. Command attention for a new topic with a strong pause.

Pauses help you gather new energy, fresh enthusiasm. They help when you momentarily lose your place or your composure. They prevent filled pauses, sometimes called word whiskers: *and huh, y'know, uh. umm.*

Pauses are your friends. Learning to be comfortable with pauses will also help you master the no eye contact, no voice rule.

Facilities Need To Be Right. Be sure that the lectern is wide enough for two full stacks of paper with no overlap. Lay the pages of your presentation on the right-hand side. As you finish each page, slide it to the left with your left hand. Reverse the stacks if you're left-handed.

If you need correcting eye wear, give your vision needs special consideration. Heavy eyeglasses are a problem: they keep slipping down your nose when you look down and you keep pushing them up, a habit distracting to both you and the audience. If you wear bifocals, consider a full frame bifocal. Having to tip back to see the pages is nerve-wracking. A CEO who gives speeches across the U.S. and internationally discovered early on that lecterns were never at quite the right height for his glasses. He bought a tiny portable music stand to take along. Now his notes are always at the right height.

Using Your Body

If you wonder about facial mannerisms, watch a videotape of a previous presentation with the sound off. See what your face does. To accentuate facial mannerisms (and all gestures) run the tape on fast forward. While appearing more animated than you actually are, your grimaces and frequent hands-about-the-face gestures will be glaringly apparent. Work to conquer those that are distracting to an audience.

A centipede was once asked which leg he started on. He thought and thought and thought about it, and was never able to walk again. Don't worry about gestures.

Don't follow the advice of a speech coach who suggested throwing smurf balls around the room to learn to duplicate the gesture of the arms. That is ridiculous.

If you have been involved in the creation of your speech, and you mean what you are saying, your voice will be expressive. Gestures will follow. Your brain wants to send gestures to complement your words. Concentrate on delivering your message; if you feel the words, the gestures will come naturally in nearly every case.

One situation in which the gestures won't come naturally is when you trap the gestures within your body (See page 45). Trapping occurs when your hands are clasped, making a closed circuit for your energy to run around on, rather than out toward the audience in a gesture. A closed circuit is created when you adopt one of these forbidden postures:

- parade rest (hands clasped behind you)
- fig leaf (hands clasped in front, at arm's length)
- flesh wound (where one hand firmly grasps the other upper arm)
- moneychanger (where your hands are protecting the money deep down inside a pocket)
- church steeple (in which your arms meet on your chest with fingers playing at that old childhood game "Here is the church…")

Solve the closed circuit problem by learning to stand in a neutral position. Arms hanging down at your sides, hands slightly flexed or curled, resting lightly on the front of your thighs. This neutral position will feel uncomfortable at first. But practicing it a few seconds at a time will soon make it comfortable. So positioned, those hands and arms rest briefly in neutral and can move freely whenever the brain sends its signal to do so. You'll quickly find that they are seldom in the neutral position; they'll be supporting your words with gestures.

POOR

BETTER

A final thought about rehearsals: Some people feel, mistakenly, that the way to sound spontaneous is by not practicing a speech very much. The absolute reverse is true. The way to sound spontaneous is to rehearse a great deal. Just looking it over on the plane on the way to the speech makes you sound unprepared and unprofessional; it makes you look unprepared and unprofessional. Preparation is everything.

You must **talk** a manuscript, not read it. You must mean it, and your voice must reflect that. You understand that it's more difficult to say it like you mean it with a manuscript than when speaking extemporaneously. But success can come if you and the speechwriter have worked together, creating words that you *do* mean and formatting it so you can deliver it with that sound.

Take-away Sentence:

It's your speech and you're responsible for it, whoever creates it.

REASON 6

"If I don't write it all out, I'll forget something."

The Problem:
Writing it all out means you'll read it. That's boring.

The Solution:
Make a good outline, get a good grasp of the material, and then talk it to the audience. Being natural is far more important than remembering everything.

What's Wrong With Writing It All Out?

Four problems persist when a speech is written out in full:

- it takes too much time to create it
- too much material is included
- the tone is usually stiff and formal
- there is seldom a structure for the audience to follow.

Creating It Takes Too Much Time. Executives who prepare their own speeches tend to sit down at their computers or their legal size yellow pads and write and write and write, pulling and pushing words around. They write it and revise it and polish it; once they get it revised and polished they think to themselves, *I'll never be able to say this as well as I've written it.* So they end up reading most of it, either from exhaustive notes or 27 note cards.

Instead of a marathon writing schedule, do the assessment described below (**The Two Percent Rule**) early. Then use your spare moments to get ideas out of your head and onto paper. Take advantage of your thought processes when you're out for a walk, swimming your laps, in the shower, driving to and from work or meetings. When a thought occurs to you, jot it down — on a yellow sticky note, a scratch paper or a cocktail napkin. Put these jottings in a folder. You can get a tremendous amount of planning done, much material gathered, without setting aside any extra time. And it's easier than writing it out.

With this folder approach you don't start from empty, with a blank sheet or a blank screen. Actually sitting down to prepare the presentation is no longer a moment to dread, because much of the raw material is assembled. Did I mention how much easier it is?

Too Much Material Is Created. People say that they write the speech out and read it because they are afraid that they will forget something. From both my professional perspectives — speech coach and professional speaker — my reaction is, **do forget something.** The chances are virtually 100% that you have more planned to say than you should say. Remember that the speech is not the whole story. You say the portion of the story appropriate for this particular audience. (Some of the story has already been given to them via other speakers, the media, brochures, marketing. Other parts of the story are dealt with during a variety of follow-up activities. That's what handouts, brochures, and pamphlets are for. That's what follow-up calls, letters, and memos are for.)

My guideline for clients is the Two Percent Rule: in a speech of an hour you will typically give no more than two percent of what you know about the topic. Two percent. Sometimes even .02 percent, depending upon your purpose and on how much of an expert you are. Once you've assessed the audience and determined your one specific purpose, it is easier to let go of the thinking that says *I've got to tell everything.* This letting go is essential to a successful, comfortable move away from a written speech.

The Tone Is Stiff. Real words genuinely spoken are more important than completeness. When you speak off the cuff, you are more natural. Your enthusiasm is more genuine. Rather than intoning the high-sounding phrases you wrote, you'll say it like you really mean it. What you lose in perfect phrases you more than make up for with the warm, candid tone you spontaneously project. You might even get excited!

The Audience Has No Structure to Follow. Let the audience know you're organized and help them follow your train of thought by providing a structure. A structure also gives you confidence to rely on your extensive knowledge and your memory. (See Reason Four for a variety of common structures for presentations.)

Do write down the structure on note cards or an agenda and take it with you. Write the key sentences: the opener, the oral guidelines (main points) and the closing. Beyond that, if you are familiar with the material, a few words should guide you through the examples and illustrations. It's easy to relate an incident or tell a story naturally, especially if you do what the pro's do, practice telling it many times.

Follow the Two Percent Rule

The most common error in presentations, from my twenty-five years' experience as a speech trainer, is speakers giving too much information. They try to cover too much. They try to tell the audience everything they know. Following the Two Percent Rule, a speech of an hour presents no more than two percent of all the knowledge a speaker has on the topic. Finding the right two percent enables you to decide what specific material belongs in the presentation and what great quantities will be left out. Remember the **Two Percent Rule,** and let it be the guide for your presentation strategies.

That's good news, because if you present two percent you have ninety-eight percent left in reserve in case your mind goes blank or the audience has other aspects it wishes to hear about. Having ninety-eight percent in reserve also creates an edge of confidence that enables you to do a superb job.

Many corporate speakers still have the mental model from high school or college speech class. Remember? You went to the library and found an encyclopedia (plus one other book or article) from which you quickly scribbled down as many notes as you could to fill the five-minute speech assignment. When you gave your speech, you knew five minutes of material plus an additional fifteen or twenty seconds' worth. You presented about ninety-eight percent of what you knew, with two percent in reserve. (Don't mind my math here.) Because you had little in reserve, you had to present everything you knew. You wrote most of the speech on note cards because you couldn't afford to forget anything.

Contrast that experience with your background as a business professional: there is a great deal that you might say; you choose the two percent that is most appropriate, given your assessment of the audience. To help determine the appropriate two percent, use the Communications Triangle in Reason Three.

Take-away Sentence:

A focused message delivered informally with genuine feeling beats a complete message which you read.

REASON 7

"My message usually covers about ten points."

The Problem:
There are two problems with making ten points:
- You probably have no focus
- You drown the audience with more information than they want or can possibly absorb.

The Solution:
Find a focus and limit your material naturally by developing a one-sentence take-away message. Then create a structure to support it.

What's Wrong With Ten Points?

Making ten points (or even six points), violate the Two Percent Rule. Ten points is usually the whole story; trying to tell the whole story is the major problem in speeches. You are asked to speak because you are the expert; you have much more knowledge than is applicable in any one speaking situation — even a workshop. This rule of thumb works: Give the beginning and the end. Skip the middle.

The quick solution is to force yourself to create a one-sentence take-away message to guide you. This sentence will then help you develop the appropriate structure.

Finding Your Structure

Most speeches are developed with the topical format: three reasons why something should be done, two approaches to the problem, four goals for a project. This topical approach is often appropriate; however, when you start writing down reasons and discover that you have ten, regroup.

Consider an instance when ten reasons turns you off. You have in hand a nice refund from the Internal Revenue Service, so you decide it's time to buy a CD player for your car. Not very sophisticated in audio-electronics, you go into the gigantic superstore somewhat hesitantly. As you stand there gazing around at the 500 television screens arrayed in front of you, all showing the same picture, a snappy young sales rep comes up with, *How may I help you today?*

A little bewildered, you respond *Oh, well, I'm sort of thinking that I might buy a CD player for my car.*

The enthusiastic rep responds, *Of course, that's wonderful. Let me show you a few of the wonderful models we have and explain some features to you.* Moving purposely over to the CD section, she begins pointing, one at a time, at ten different models, rapidly spilling out statistics and features. At the end of her long spiel, she asks, *Any questions?* Totally bewildered, you are likely to respond, *Oh, no thanks, I'm just looking,* and walk out of the store. That sales person tried to tell you everything she knew. She also failed to identify **you** (not herself) as the person the message was for. She also said what she wanted to say, rather than what you needed to hear. Keep this story in mind when you have trouble cutting down to two or three main points.

Remember, again, that the presentation is only two percent of the story, not the whole story. It's part of a larger picture. Your task is to identify the particular part of the picture that is appropriate at this point for this audience. The most frequent development plan has two or three topical points — not ten.

Options to the Topical Structure

With the topical structure — three reasons, two goals — it's too easy to expand to four, six, eight, ten reasons. Another way to help overcome the **My speeches usually contain about ten points** problem is selecting another structural approach. Others are often more appropriate and easier to organize. Look at your material. Look at your purpose. Look at your audience. Then consider one of these four other common approaches for your organizational structure:

- chronological
- spatial
- problem solving
- need-fulfillment.

A **chronological** development plan, using a time frame or time line, begins in the past, moving to the present, then on to the future. You describe the opening days of a project, continuing through the second phase, and on to the final phase. Perhaps its the before and after of a particular project; or the "how we used to do it" compared to "how we do it now"; six steps for development of a plan — all of these invite a chronological structure. If you have a chronological topic, this structure literally organizes itself.

Another organizational structure is **spatial**. This structure lends itself to physical items or geographic locations. It presents material from the front to the back, from the inside to the outside, from the top to the bottom, from suburban to urban, from California to New York. Physical items or geographical topics which lend themselves to spatial organization tend to have a logical order. If there does not appear to be a logical order, if the items or locations could be talked about in any order, go back to the perspective of your audience. Decide which order would be most logical from their perspective. It's not what will make sense to you that matters, it's what will make sense to this audience.

A third organizational structure for development is **problem solving**. This is generally a three-part presentation: demonstrate that a problem exists, attribute the causes, and then propose a solution. Assess the background knowledge of the audience carefully. Much of the desire to tell too much rests here. Many times the section which demonstrates the problem can be brief, because the audience is familiar with the problem.

The fourth organizational structure is **need-fulfillment**. Begin the presentation by creating a need or desire or describing a need or desire that the audience already has. In the second part, propose a method to fill that need. This is a common organizational plan for sales presentations. Knowledge of your audience is vital to accurately describe the need or desire. Thorough knowledge of your service or product helps you propose a method to fulfill that desire or need. Be careful to describe the fulfillment in terms of its benefits to the audience, not in terms of its features. (See Reason Eight for more on using benefits rather than features in your presentation.)

Though seventy-five percent of speeches use a topical structure, these are hardest to limit to Two Percent. One of these four alternate organizational plans will frequently be easier to narrow and a better vehicle for your message.

Why an Organizational Plan Matters

Having an organizational plan is important because it lets you know that you're in control. It's a structure that guides all your design, including expanding the support points and creating your visual aids.

Equipped with a one-sentence message and a structure, you won't be thrown by an unexpected change. It's easy to comply when asked to shorten your speech. For one thing, you have an **elevator** speech prepared: You find yourself standing next to a decision-maker in the elevator, with the ride time of ten floors to make your point. With the one sentence message and the structure, you can make the most of the elevator ride!

Or you expect to make your pitch in a calm, well-timed presentation; the decision maker comes up to you beforehand with this comment, *I'm going to have to miss your presentation, John. Give me the highlights.* You can give them easily.

Or as you arrive for your sales proposal, the chairperson greets you with this heart stopper, *I'm sorry, we're running terribly behind. You've got only five minutes instead of the fifteen we promised you. Will that be all right?* Your response is a calm, *Of course,* because you can deliver the essence easily, with impact.

Narrowing Your Material

Narrow your material by having fewer facts, less logic, and more illustrative material. Use stories and examples as the body of the speech. Let the examples prove the rule. A government employee asked for assistance in preparing a twenty-minute presentation for a national audience. The presentation was an update on three different programs that she had been instrumental in developing for seven regions around the U.S. The conference officials had thoughtfully provided her with a list of items she might cover. It was a gigantic list of stuff. She and I quickly agreed that such a presentation, reporting on all the items on the list for each program for every region would be deadly dull.

We decided that the purpose of the presentation was building goodwill, a morale booster. We drew up a one-sentence message, highlighting the excitement of change. The support material would consist of one real life success story for each of the three programs. She could thus include three of the regions specifically. Her ability to relate stories would add sparkle and vigor to the presentation; the enthusiasm of success stories insured a dynamite presentation.

But you're still wrestling with the desire to tell all that you know, to squeeze in every single possible fact and detail. Will it help you to know that eliminating excess material is difficult to achieve, even for speakers at the professional level? Let me walk you through the evolution of the basic speech from my third book, *How to Talk So Men Will Listen*. I have given this speech several hundred times. The take-away sentence was, "Say less than you want to say." For the first fifty or sixty speeches, there were seven main points:

- Special communications situations require special techniques
- It's a gender issue
- It's a power issue
- Feel like an equal
- Act like an equal
- Sound like an equal
- Look like an equal.

My speech developed these points with statistics, some theory, a few stories and examples. Because I'm a professional, I guess I fancied that I could be successful with it, giving lots and lots of content. (Does this thinking sound familiar?) I rationalized, just as you do, that because people came to hear this subject they wanted to know as much as they possibly could. It was successful, because I kept being asked back.

Mindful of what I coach others to do, however, I kept the same take-away message but moved gradually to three main points: "It's a gender issue," "It's a power issue," and "It's an equality issue." The four equalities — feel, act, sound, and look — remained, but became subpoints. Cutting the number of bullets meant cutting out some of the detail and adding more stories. The speech became lighter and funnier. People liked it a great deal.

The speech has evolved with the subtitle *Reeducating Rita: A Fable for the Nineties Woman.* There are seven bullets, but the hard content for each bullet is a single sentence, the supporting content for each is a story. The seven bullets are:

- Say less than you want to say
- Ask for what you want
- Give your opinion
- Act like an equal
- Feel like an equal
- Sound like an equal
- Look like an equal.

Instead of detail and reasons, nearly all the content is funny, real stories to illustrate each point. It's the version of the speech that the audience most enjoys hearing and the one I most enjoy giving. It's the best of the three basic iterations. Using stories as the main support creates more humor, encouraging vocal variety in characterizations. Audiences adore it!

Just like you, I used to try to tell it all. I changed. I recognized that what I coach and teach other to do **works**. Skill in delivery was no excuse to tell the whole story.

Getting to the Point

The major task for speakers is to choose the right two percent. Your structure is the framework of key sentences, facts or opinions, stated clearly and forcefully. Make fewer main points and give less detail, filling the time with interesting content. Use stories, examples, anecdotes, illustrations, and analogies.

Use interesting, effective stories. Stories have many values:

- stories are easily remembered
- stories provide structure or organize a series of ideas
- stories are a safe place to talk about complex ideas or issues
- stories create a sense of togetherness
- stories engage the imagination
- stories encourage listening (John Ward, *The Toastmaster*, August 1990).

Share real experiences. Develop a file of anecdotes to draw upon. An anecdote is a brief account of a real incident in a person's life. Questions create anecdotes: Someone asks, *How did you invent this product?* and an anecdote leaps out: *My wife and I made the first crude version of it in our kitchen one rainy Saturday....* Find client success stories, stories which demonstrate product development, stories about incidents that motivated an idea for better service. Include calls from customers with actual requests and complaints. People remember stories. If the audience remembers the stories, they'll remember the points.

Here are some other suggestions for interesting supporting content.

A 1000 Word Picture. Use vivid description to paint a picture with words that your audience can vividly "see." If you need to, use an actual picture as your inspiration and as your practice vehicle. The picture may be of a secluded high mountain lake which is endangered by a construction project; a lively child whose well-being is threatened by a potential school levy defeat; a frail elderly parent who is in need of adult day care. Tug at people's heartstrings a bit. Search for vocabulary with active energetic verbs, crisp adjectives.

Two Pictures of 500 Words Each. Paint a contrast; the before and after of a spoiled environmental feature; a sick child/well child contrast following contributions to a fund drive; a vacant lot/cheery playground scenario for the neighborhood; a trashy lot/green fingers garden for a depressed area.

"War" Stories. Involve the audience with an extended story from your experience which illustrates a point of the talk. Get down to the small details of description; remember (or invent) some dialogue between two opposite individuals. Use funny voices if you can carry them off.

Talk about a tough time and how you overcame it. Let them share your experience so that they too are moved to tears or laughter by its retelling.

Clean, Simple Jokes That You Individualize to Your Point. Yes, there are some jokes you can use, but not many and virtually never at the beginning of your speech. (See Reason Nine for more on use of jokes.)

Jokes need to be clean and simple. They need to be easy to tell, and you need to have told them many times so that they are practiced well. Most important, they cannot insult anybody, because the chances are good that a joke will insult someone in your audience. Second, they need to be closely tied to material, so you don't have to make the point. In the 20+ years I've been giving speeches and training about communicating, I've developed about six jokes which relate to my topics — communications. Each is squeaky clean; each can be individualized with a town or street name. Here's a brief version of one, which I use to reinforce the need to say *exactly* what you mean, not *sort of* what you mean:

> A police officer is out on a major surface street, using his radar. He pulls over an old green Valiant. As he approaches he notices that the back seat is filled with penguins. As he finishes writing and hands over the ticket, he adds in a firm voice, "And I want you to take those penguins to the zoo."
>
> A week later, same police officer, same street, same speeding green Valiant. Officer notices the penguins are still in the back seat, but this time they are wearing sun glasses. He hands the ticket through the window and remarks somewhat testily, "I thought I told you to take those penguins to the zoo!" The driver timidly responds, "But, Officer, I did. And we had such a good time, today we're all going to the beach."

This is a sample of a joke that meets all the requirements. The only people who could be insulted would be drivers of old cars or penguin lovers, and neither group is apt to be insulted by the joke. Does it make fun of police officers? Apparently not. I used the joke in a speech for a conference of police officers, and they got a huge laugh out of it.

This short piece of humor set me up as the unmechanical person that I am for a speech to a society of design engineers: *I'm not mechanical; I don't even know how kleenex works. I pull one and another is right there. It must have something to do with the box, though, because when I took them out the box they didn't pop up any more.*

If it's necessary to use a lecture format, this is my favorite line: *I'm here to instruct and you're here to learn. If you finish before I do, please let me know.*

Analogies make complicated topics understandable and memorable. An environmental speaker attempting to get her audience to understand the concept of parts per million used this analogy: *An old Indian chieftain, sweaty from a long horseback ride, jumped into the lake to clean off. The amount of salt from his sweat still in the water after 200 years would be one part per million.* She also indicated that one part per million is one second in thirty five thousand years.

You can turn impossible-to-imagine quantities into memorable information with analogies: People in the United States bought 60 million muffins last year, enough lined up next to each other to form a line from Seattle to Boston, and on down to Miami.

Technical information can be made non-technical with similes. A marine scientist, when referring to the unique markers (called scents) that distinguish each sea anemone, said, *They are as unique as a social security number, or a scent that lets a dog track its owner through a circus.*

Need to Know Information. The old sales triad, Need to Know, Nice to Know, and Don't Need to Know, is a useful device for helping you separate material for any specific audience. For an example of the triad in decision-making, consider a report of an activity. There are two primary types of reports you could give. One is an historical report (what I call the "and then we..." report), the other is a results-focused or "bottom line" report.

In any event there are several key questions: *What happened? When did it happen? Who was involved? Why did it happen? What were the results? What will the repercussions be?* The good speaker (or writer) divides the information into three categories: Need To Know, Nice To Know, and Don't Need To Know.

In an historical report (the kind that long-winded speakers tend to give), all these aspects are mentioned and many are thoroughly described. The speaker seldom attempts to differentiate between the important and the trivial: it all comes out equally.

In a results-oriented speech most attention is given to the final two questions, *Why did it happen? What are the repercussions?* These are the bottom line. The speaker takes it upon herself to decide the "Need-to-Know" information. The "Nice-to-Know" details will be available if they are requested during the Q & A. The "Don't-Need-to-Know" tidbits are just that.

Remember that selecting an organizational plan is one step in creating the structure. (Developing oral guidelines is the other; see Reason Four.)

Take-away Sentence:

Cover two or three points interestingly, rather than ten points jammed with facts.

REASON 8

"We're selling a product. Of course we talk mostly about features."

The Problem:
  People buy benefits, not features.

The Solution:
  Whether your presentation is "selling" a service, a product, or an idea, create success by emphasizing how it will benefit the audience.

What's the Matter With Features?

Wanting to talk about features is natural, because you know and understand your product or service; besides that, it's easy to talk about features. For even the best presenters, the basic corporate speech is typically filled with *we, us,* and *our.* The basic problem with this approach is that members of your audience are interested in themselves. The speech should be filled with *you* and *your.* Presentations are essentially selling; it may be an idea, a concept, a belief, or a cause; often it's your company, a product, or a service. You're selling. You're asking your audience to buy. People buy benefits. They justify their purchase with features, but it's the benefits that convince them.

Consider purchases made in preparation for a cold winter. A Minnesotan doesn't select a new wool cap because it's made of 100 percent wool, half llama and half lambs wool, with flaps that come down over the ears, in 17 bright plaid patterns. These are features. She buys it because it will keep her ears warm and match her coat. These are benefits.

Whatever your topic, make the distinction between features and benefits, then be certain your speech is benefits-oriented.

Finding Benefits-Oriented Language

There is an easy test for language that's benefits-oriented. Assume the audience is prepared to challenge your every word. Visualize the audience sitting in front of you, arms folded, leaning back, responding to each of your utterances with *So?* Your goal is to change their posture, their language, and their attitude. Get them leaning forward in their chairs, responding *Ohhh!*

Here's an example: you represent a financial planning company. You stand up and proudly begin,

> *We have been serving clients like you for 27 years.*
> [The audience is thinking, *So?*]

> *We have nine cross-trained analysts to help you with every phase of your investment.*
> [*So?*]

Our analysts are all cross-trained so that they can move your money back and forth between stocks and bonds. [Who cares?]

Hmmm. This is not the response you want. You must be talking features, not benefits. Here are the key statements recast with benefits-oriented language:

Your money will get the highest return because our cross trained staff can move it from stocks to bonds when necessary.
[Hmmm.]

For 27 years people like you have seen their money grow with us.
[Ohhh!]

You get the idea. Don't just say what you **want** to say. Say what the audience **needs** to hear, or wants to hear. What they need or want to hear is benefits. Almost everything you are accustomed to describing as a feature of your company, product, or service can be recast as a benefit to your audience. That's the language that you aim for.

Setting the Tone With the Opener

Set the tone and the perspective for a benefits-oriented message with the opener (the first sentence you speak.) The language should be *you*, not *I* or *we*. *You* signals that you will focus on what the audience needs or wants. An appropriate pronoun in the opener is the first step in finding language that creates a benefits-laden message.

Here's another easy test for benefits-laden language. Remember your high school grammar? The subject word of the sentence is the most important word in the sentence. To assess whether your language is benefits-oriented, check the subject words in the sentences in your speech. *You will find peace of mind with this plan. Your **health** is your most important asset. Your **safety** is our first concern. Your **comfort** determines what your decision should be. Your **retirement money** will grow with this plan* — these subject words indicate that what you're saying is what audiences want to hear, a benefits-oriented speech.

The glossy four-color promotional brochure of an engineering client of mine includes a page which they also translate to speeches. The page is headed *Client-Centered Service*. The key line begins appropriately: ***Client-centered service** is what distinguishes XYZ Corporation from other engineering firms.* The text reads, in part, *At XYZ Corporation, **we** provide value to **our** clients in two ways: **our** professional service, what **we** do, and the client-centered service, how **we** do it. **We** want **our** clients to consider XYZ Corporation as noticeably superior in all respects. **Our** professionalism, the quality of **our** services, and how **we** treat clients....* I'll stop there, because you get the point. The title says *client-centered*, but the profusion of *we* and *our* pronouns let the reader know that the firm is actually *firm-centered*, that it is *features-oriented* rather than benefits-oriented.

You do need to include features; learn to weave them in. For example, here are features:

> *We've been in business for nine years. We have over a million users. We have 85 percent market share. We have six offices worldwide.*

Weave the features in to show how the prospect can sell the product to her end users:

Because there are over a million users of this software, your customers know the product pleases its users....

Because we have six offices worldwide, you will be able to offer follow-up service....

You get the idea.

Examine your presentations (and your written material). If they're features-oriented, recast that material into benefits-oriented language. Remember it's not what you want to say but what the audience needs or wants to hear that matters.

Your goal is to move the unspoken reaction of your audience from *So* and *Who cares?* to *Ohhh.* Once you've moved them to *Ohhh,* they're paying attention.

Take-away Sentence:

Audiences get your message easier

when you talk about them than

when you talk about you.

REASON 9

"We begin our presentations with our biography."

The Problem:

Beginning with your name and information about your company is boring and features-oriented, not benefits-oriented.

The Solution:

Plan an opener that grabs the attention of the audience. Plan a question, a benefit, a statistic, or a challenge that compels the audience to tune in.

What's Wrong With Our Bio?

The goal of the opener is capturing the attention of the audience immediately. Beginning with some information about yourself or your company seldom accomplishes that vital task. What draws the audience to you is an opener about them.

Problem — Boring Opener Which Talks About Yourself. Does this opener sound familiar?

Good morning, I'm Shawn Kemper, and I'm president of Professional Consolidated Services. It's a real pleasure to be here in Des Moines today to share with you some of the ideas I have about how customer service can be improved. Because you're here, I assume you want to provide better customer service and I can help you do that.

or,

Thank you, Ralph, for that wonderful introduction. As Ralph said, I am John Smith of Markquar Corporation. What I thought we'd do this morning is talk about...

Here's another biographical opener of the type to avoid:

I want to alter the format of this presentation today. At the previous three or four meetings, I have focused on quarterly performance, and I realize that some of the material has been "dry." Today I really want to take a few minutes to discuss how I'm feeling about the company and what we're doing, going forward. My remarks will include a discussion of goals and objectives, and a description of current activities in each of our three business segments, consistent with these goals.

In all three samples the audience is thinking, *So? We don't care about your ancient history. What about US?* The major problems are 1) you won't capture the attention of the listeners because they're boring openers, and 2) you send a signal that you will talk about yourself or your company instead of about them (see Reason Eight).

Problem — Boring Opener That Talks About Your Company. Equally unsuccessful is the opener which spends the first few minutes talking about one's own company before moving on to the topic or the industry. Here's a sample:

Good morning, it's a real pleasure to be here this morning, and I am delighted to share with you Johnson Company's perspective on railroad highlights for the nineties. Our company, the Johnson Company, was founded in 1934 by our esteemed founder, Howard H. Johnson, who believed, even back then, that the railroad was going to be the best, cheapest means of transporting people and goods that we could possibly come up with. Our company, in business since 1934, last year broke sales records with blah, blah... Our company has grown from the five employees that Mr. Johnson gathered around him, to 50,000 employees in ten regional centers across the United States.

Boring.

Problem — Failure to Recognize Speech Purpose. The boring biographical beginning is particularly typical for a corporate president or VP of marketing representing the company at a trade or industry show. Why do speakers create these boring opener? Why do speech writers do this to speakers? Primarily because they don't recognize that there are two purposes for the speech: the one the industry show has in mind, and your own. The speech preparer sees it as another marketing opportunity. And it is. But the marketing must be subtle, because the audience didn't come to hear your marketing pitch. They have come for your take on conditions in the industry. You can include your marketing pitch by weaving it in.

Problem — Thinking That Credibility Needs To Be Established. People create company backgrounds as openers to establish credibility; they believe they need to present their credentials. Such speakers don't give themselves or their company sufficient credit for reputation in the industry. If you or your company is well enough known to be asked to present, you're well enough known to get on with it.

Clients say, *Well, yes, but I'd really like to get in a few things about our company.* Of course you would. Learn to weave them in to the presentation. You may weave in statistics, some of your biographical background, company information, even what the founder said. Just don't make them a separate section that stands out at the beginning like a great sore thumb.

Problem — Too Much Ancient History. Another mistake that speakers and speech writers make when they're creating an opener is going too far back in history, using the chronological approach: *We were founded... for sixteen years..., then..., and now we're....* To counteract the inclination to create this approach, remind yourself, *We're industry leaders. People know that. We don't have to explain or justify or keep beating our drum about how successful we are.* Get to the point.

Another ancient history problem in openers occurs after your company has spun-off or become a subsidiary of a larger company. Just after the change, it's natural to begin with information about your parent company. But three or five years later, a million or five million dollars in sales later, people either already know about your origins, or else it doesn't matter. Reliance on one's parentage sends a signal you still aren't sure of your corporate identity.

Chronological approaches are not very successful anyway, because people want to know, *What have you done lately?* Start with the punch line. Then if you feel that you must go back to some history, flash back to it.

Problem — Out-of-Context Company Results. Sometimes current company results get highlighted in the opener. A speaker relates last year's results, future projections, plans for this year, year-to-date performance. Isolated at the beginning of the speech, this information has no frame of reference. Since the audience doesn't know what to do with the information, they are turned off by it. They quit listening and start doodling.

Creating an Effective Opener

The opener is the most important sentence in the entire speech. These are the first words out of your mouth. Strong content and power will draw the attention of the listeners; your name, your biography, your thanks, will not achieve that end. Before you begin, the audience anticipates you, expecting, and hoping, you'll do well. Your task is to capitalize on that expectation with a meaningful opener. And don't risk giving away the power of your carefully prepared opener by responding to what an introducer said or what a previous speaker said — unless a gross misconception needs to be corrected.

Consider the opener as a hook to catch or capture the minds of the audience. When you begin to speak, no matter what group it is, only one person in the room has his or her mind on the topic of the day — you. Everyone else is thinking about something else — how hot it is, how much work she has set aside to come to the session, his sick child, her angry boss, his irritated client. Even if you're the president and it's your staff, nobody's mind is fully on the topic.

Your opening sentence moves those minds from their thoughts onto your topic. Usually, the opener should consist of words directly related to your material. Here are seven possibilities for openers:

- the clear one-sentence message
- a question
- an autobiographical comment
- a statistic
- a quotation
- a dramatic or vital statement
- a descriptive opener.

The Clear One-sentence Message. Opening with your carefully developed one-sentence message works — especially if you deliver it powerfully. It is, after all, the one sentence you want the audience to take away. It's well crafted, it's precise, and you can deliver it dynamically. It's a wonderful opener.

Or choose some other hook to get the audience's attention, to arouse their curiosity. Follow with your one-sentence message.

A Question. A question is my personal favorite for the hook because, phrased in the second person, it forces the audience to think about the topic just for a second. *Do you ever...? How many times have you...? What's your first thought when you hear the word...?* This opener requires mental involvement. Even they don't want to think about the question, they're already hooked. (For ways to use the opening questions for even further involvement, see Reason Fourteen.)

Asking a series of closely related, brief, and well-timed questions grabs the audience.

An Autobiographical Comment. Talk about yourself. But be careful: An autobiographical comment can easily become boring by going on too long. Because we all like to talk about ourselves, it's easy to get too involved.

On the plus side, an autobiographical comment helps the audience identify with you. If you're speaking as an expert, for instance, sharing details about yourself can be a great help. You might begin an address to a professional group of consultants this way: *Having just completed my fifteenth year as a management consultant, I've learned one key lesson: being an expert is hard work!*

Use an autobiographical comment that indicates "we're in this together": *Most of you have worked for this company even longer than I have. Saving it must be our priority.*

Another caution with the autobiographical opener: it's too easy to fall right into the *Hello, My name is John Smith* trap. Speakers feel impelled to reveal some biographical data. One said, *But I should tell them who I am and where I've come from, what my expertise is.* Perhaps. Usually not, at least directly. Your credibility was established by the person who invited you to speak. [The better approach for working in your background is to weave it in throughout your presentation. Make a list of four or five credentials — background, prominent client names, experience — the audience should know, and weave them into the fabric of your speech. Here's my list of background to weave into a speech to the Montana Agribusiness Association:

- I was born on a farm.
- I'm originally from Idaho, a neighboring farm state.

- I've been working in communications for 30 years.
- Among my clients are the Western Agricultural Chemical Association, J.R. Simplot, and Lamb Weston.

As I prepare my notes, these four personal items will find a spot. For example, *When I was helping the people at Lamb Weston with their customer services goals, the question arose....* Using the client name as a part of my support carries much more weight than it would if I had simply named them as clients in my introduction. Another weaving in of those credentials: *In the thirty years I've been speaking on the subject of customer service to groups such as yours, this concern has come up more than any other....* or *At the Western Ag Chem meeting that many of you also attended last year, we discussed....* You get the idea.] Make your credentials work harder for you and make them more interesting to the audience by weaving them into your speech rather than beginning with them.

A Statistic, Quotation, Dramatic or Vital Statement. All of these fall in the same category — a device to jolt people, to startle them. Such a hook engages their minds because of the immensity of the number, the tremendous quality of the quotation, the gripping nature of the vital statement.

As an undergraduate at the University of Idaho many years ago I recall a presentation by an environmentalist. As students in the early 1960s, we didn't even know what an environmentalist was. We had no idea what to expect from this speaker.

He strode into the room, slapped a stack of thick books loudly onto the table in front of the nine of us, and slowly intoned in a deep, resonant voice: *Within twenty years, three out of the ten people in this room will be dead from the effects of environmental pollution.* Did he ever get our attention! We each must have thought to ourselves *Wow! Am I one of the three?* His delivery style, tone and manner complemented his words perfectly. He had us literally in the palm of his hand.

How can you pick a question, a statistic, a quotation, a vital statement which will hook your audience? By understanding what motivates them. See "Assessing the Audience" in Reason Three.

A Descriptive Opener. Description is effective and also fun to do if you have some imagination and can develop a scene (either real or imagined) with descriptive language. You might begin a descriptive opener by saying, *Visualize... Imagine that you... Picture....* Describe a place that you have been or a situation you've been involved in which fits the motivation of your audience. Quality of description is the key: Make it lively and visual so the audience gets a sharp mental picture as you are talking.

The goal of the opener is to grab your audience by the lapels, get them to sit up and say, *Ohh!* right away.

What About Jokes?

Notice that there is not an opener called a joke. That's because jokes are generally not successful openers. You know this. You have heard speakers tell jokes that embarrassed you, affronted you, offended your dignity, made someone in the audience downright angry. You've heard jokes that didn't come off. These failures are followed by a pained silence. The audience is uncomfortable for themselves and for the speaker. The speaker is uneasy with himself. People assume that jokes are ice-breakers; the truth is they break much more than ice.

There are so many problems with telling a joke and so few things right about it, that I recommend never using jokes as openers unless you are a professional humorist. First, jokes generally depend on making fun of somebody or something for their humor; it's extremely difficult to tell a joke which does not insult someone in your audience. You can't afford to risk that.

A joke also is not a successful opener because it is difficult to tell one well. Professional speakers typically practice a joke or story forty or fifty times before they use it in a presentation. Even if you manage to tell a joke successfully, it seldom relates closely enough to your material that you can move smoothly into your point. You tell the joke and everybody laughs, and then you say, *But seriously, folks...?* That doesn't work.

A variation of the joke as opener is an entire introduction — usually written by speech writers — that tries to be humorous. Humor is very difficult to communicate. It seems good on paper. It seems good if you're saying it out loud to one other person, but like a joke, it comes off differently in front of a group. I vividly remember a speech in which the speaker tried humor of the self-deprecating kind, putting himself down. Though safe, because it isn't making fun of others, it's the most difficult kind of humor to carry off. It requires mastery at timing and intonation. This "humorous" introduction went like this:

> *Historians say that those who listened to John Wesley's stirring sermons often were moved to quote "shed tears, falling into fits, and crying out hysterically." Some of my remarks have the same effect —*

[pause] — But I'm trying to improve, and it seems to be working. My last speech was quite moving. By the time I finished, most of the audience had moved to another room, though.

What one speaker in ten thousand can carry off that kind of humor? This one wasn't one of them. It was embarrassing, not funny.

Another speaker who began his presentation with what he apparently thought was an obligatory stand-up comedy routine subjected his audience to this groaner:

Thank you very much, Martha, for the wonderful introduction. I'm reminded of something that happened yesterday when I was coming in from the airport. My driver was a small fellow with a big black mustache, and a South-of-the-Border accent. When I told him I was going to speak to you today, he turned to me and said — now I'm not sure I can get the accent right, but here goes — He turned to me and said, "Leesten, Senor. Leesten...."

Some jokes will fit into your material; learn to tell them well. Humor can be successful during the body of a presentation, especially humor directed at yourself or arising naturally from your material.

Yet another opener which is difficult to carry off is building to a mini-climax, taking four or five minutes to get to the point. This approach is difficult because of the need for great timing and vocal control and because audiences are not as patient as they used to be. In this inductive approach, the speaker moves from point to point to point, finally getting to the punch line or key idea. Often, people use quotations, headlines from magazines, or statistics to build to an irrepressible, irrefutable climax. It can be done if the quotes, statistics, or headlines are each in themselves interesting and if each is delivered with such compelling style that the audience is sitting on the edges of its chairs, literally waiting for the next one. Not easy.

This inductive building approach is typically part of a manuscript presentation. The take-away sentence would be at the end of the third or fourth page. It's extremely difficult to keep an audience interested and involved long enough to reach the bottom of the fourth page.

What about "Good Morning"?

What's wrong with *Good Morning?* It's old. Nobody listens. Nobody cares. You make no connection. Also resist the urge to begin with *It's good to be here…. Thanks for that wonderful introduction, Janice…. Thanks for having me.* They are tired old beginnings. These cliches or platitudes are so common that nobody listens to them. They will continue contentedly with their own thoughts until you rouse them, if you still can.

It is also difficult to deliver these old chestnuts with any degree of enthusiasm or excitement. A speaker who tries to sound enthusiastic with *Good morning* sounds phony or foolish.

What about starting with your name? No built-in excitement there, I regret to say. It's a Catch-22: If you are a famous person, the audience already knows you; if you aren't famous, your name won't get the desired result, rapt attention. Besides your name is generally listed in the program; sometimes the introducer also gives your name: *Please help me welcome John Smith.* And yet haven't you heard some dim soul begin his talk following that exact introduction with, *Hello, I'm John Smith?*

If you feel compelled to name yourself, do so at some later point in your introduction — anyplace but the opener. For example, in a talk before an community group, this might be your opener: *You have one last chance to preserve some of your heritage! You have one last opportunity to make a difference in the environment for your grandchildren!... Good afternoon, I'm Helena Jones, with three suggestions for making the most of this last opportunity.*

Getting a Good Introduction

What if someone is going to introduce you? Write an introduction for the person to use. Most people will be delighted because it saves them having to figure out what to say. Additionally there will be less chance for the usual problems:

- giving away your punch line
- taking too much of your speaking time
- boring the audience with a routine
- giving you such a buildup you can never live up to it.

Avoid at all costs a laundry list of your education or work experience. These items are too often standard in an introduction prepared by someone other than you.

How long should the introduction be? About four sentences. What should it include? Some people want only their name: *Please help me give a big Montana welcome to Marian Woodall.* More likely you will include a hint about your topic, plus aspects of your background which create a quick connection with the audience. Select one or two items which reflect why you are speaking — you won an award, wrote a book, or are a recognized industry expert. Sometimes these items connect you to the audience geographically; sometimes they connect you with technical or industry expertise.

Take-away Sentence:

An opener demanding the attention of the audience magnifies your chances of success in the rest of the speech.

REASON 10

"We repeat the points from our written proposal."

The Problem:
Repeating the points from your written proposal is a problem for several reasons:

- You waste the opportunity to present another approach to the topic.
- You waste the opportunity to demonstrate teamwork, communicating skills, people skills, and chemistry.
- You waste time, because people can absorb that information, especially the details, at another time.
- You insult the audience, most of whom can read, and some of whom **have** read your proposal.

The Solution:
Recognize that the oral portion of a proposal has a different purpose from the written portion. Present different material in a different way to project the special qualities of your team or organization.

Why Do Oral Proposals Need a Different Approach?

Consider a bid for a project. You submit a written presentation responding to the RFP, detailing your credentials for the work. This presentation may be either formal or casual. Maybe you send a letter, maybe you prepare a complete package. Your firm is then asked to come in with an oral presentation. Repeating the essentials of your written proposal in that session is a waste of time and effort. And the reason is obvious: you have already made the short list. Your credentials are no longer in question. If your credentials are not in question, there's no point in repeating them.

And if your firm is invited to make an oral presentation as the first part of a bid, you have still been selected to the short list and your credentials are not in question.

Such mindless repetition is also squandering a wonderful opportunity. Ask yourself, *What is the purpose of the oral?* Your prospective clients want to know if they can work with you. They want to find out more about your approach, work methods, internal processes. They'd like some first hand accounts of how you handle problems. They want to watch your team at work. They want to check on personalities and to observe the chemistry between your group and their group.

Your assessment of the audience is especially important. Find out as much as you can about who will be present. Two areas of concern are 1) Who are the players and what are they like? 2) What's the personality or culture of the organization? Learn all you can about the individuals and what they represent in the organization, (accounting, marketing, public relations, directors, staff). Ask questions about what the firm likes and what they're looking for;

then develop a creative oral presentation that demonstrates two points: you know what they're looking for, and you can deliver it.

Grabbing the Chance To Be Creative

Here's an example of how the creative approach works. A public relations firm was getting ready to make an oral presentation, following their written proposal. They were on the short list of a project that would bring together the often conflicting agendas of several distinct business units within the client company. The project was two-fold: build a consensus among these diverse business units, and then generate public involvement that would be highly controversial. As an added point of potential difficulty, the PR firm had done virtually no work for that particular industry; however, this firm felt confident that their skill sets were equal to the task.

Their typical approach in the past had been the same old recasting of the written material. They wanted to use their twenty minutes in some creative way to demonstrate that

1) they truly understood the ramifications of the problem, and
2) they had the skills and the style to deal with the industry, even though they had no prior experience in it.

Here's the way we developed that creative presentation. The presenters, the PR group, figuratively sat in the chairs of their prospective clients and asked themselves, *If we were the clients what would we like to hear? What do we need to know to help us make a decision about whether this is the right firm for us?*

That discussion evolved five questions phrased from the client's perspective:

1. *Do you know what you're getting into?*
2. *Do you understand what will happen in-house?*
3. *Can you deal with the diverse personalities in our company?*
4. *Can you handle the public?*
5. *Can you take the heat?*

These five questions provided the structure for their oral presentation.

Next they examined ways to answer those questions, demonstrating both their experience and their skill in similar situations. They dredged up stories, examples, and illustrations which showcased their skills. The team members in the presenting firm established what needed to be done to make the project successful, weaving in, client names and experiences. They would demonstrate teamwork by fielding discussion and questions from the prospects with no sense of interruptions.

The presenting team was excited and enthusiastic. The approach met their exacting objectives. They created a check list to be sure they weren't including the same points from their written proposal. Once beyond the initial apprehension of breaking the old mold, they resolved to make a fresh approach for every oral presentation, no matter how this one turned out.

Their approach was daring, and at first glance, it seemed quite risky because the instructions had been precise. The letter requesting the oral presentation had clearly stated, *Spend about ten minutes giving us your background, describe similar engagements you have worked on... and be sure to leave time for questions and answers.*

This team, having the strength of its convictions and being inspired by the enthusiasm we created beforehand, resolved to tackle this precise command head on. The president would say in her opening remarks, *In spite of your instructions, we've chosen to present to you a living example of the kind of work that you will get from us; we are confident that by the end it will be clear why you should hire us.* The five questions were on story boards, to direct the discussion.

Well, it went beautifully. They were practiced, they were prepared, they were excited. They won the account and doubled their resolve to never go back to the old way of just repeating the main points from the written presentation.

Did They Read the Written Proposal? A client will say to me, *Yes, but we repeat the written information because we think they probably haven't read it.* That's their problem, isn't it? Somebody read it. Your firm is on the short list, after all. Don't do their thinking for them. Your goal for the oral is to create enough trust, confidence, enthusiasm, or excitement that they will read it later, if they still need to. If you present the same information and the clients recognize this material as the same old stuff, because they did read it, that's *your* problem.

Breaking the Mold — Can Your Firm Do It?

The traditional approach for orals in most industries is to have the managing partner, president, or CEO say a few words about how excited they are to be able to present to this firm and then introduce the team members. Each team member has a little piece in which he or she talks about a particular area of expertise and then names a few clients, to indicate background and experience. Of course most of this is already in the written proposal, in a section titled Client Experience, or Background, and in the Resume section.

Following the bio + clients portion, the spokesperson CEO comes back in and says, *Are there any questions we might answer for you?* Then there's a little summary, and it's done. Boring.

What should you do? Recognize what a wonderful opportunity you have to break the mold. Seize the opportunity to present your company as you work. Don't just state you know how to do something, demonstrate those skills in action.

Do not be afraid to violate the traditional approach. Are you taking a risk to do something different from what you usually do? Perhaps, but not as big a risk as you think. In work with firms which prepare proposals, including architecture, office design, accounting, public relations, and financial management, once I suggest an opportunity to cover new ground rather than just replowing the old ground, they see the logic of it. They respond with enthusiasm, and they have success.

What Works

Show rather than just telling. Reveal yourselves and your own corporate culture. Let your personalities and your enthusiasm be reflected in your approach and your tone. Use your oral presentation time to demonstrate a particular skill set which the project will require. Here are two brief examples.

Demonstrate Teamwork. Demonstrating teamwork is crucial when a project will require frequent interaction with your client. Showing that you understand teamwork and can get the others comfortably involved **by actually doing it** makes a much stronger case than just stating you are good at it.

Demonstrate Problem Solving. If there will be problem solving between your team and the prospect's team in the project, demonstrate that you understand the strategies of problem solving and that you've done it, by actually problem solving during the oral presentation. Visualize a project which will require a good deal of initial interaction between your team and the company team to determine the problems and establish parameters. Consider approaching the oral presentation as a brainstorming session which actively involves your team and their team. Demonstrate how you work by working. Show instead of just telling.

Since your decision to be bolder depends on who the prospect is, assessing the audience is of utmost importance (See Reason Two). At first glance, a bank might not seem to be the kind of prospect to be bold with. But in examining their advertising campaign, you recognize their ad people are being extremely creative, so they're not opposed to inventiveness and ingenuity. You know a couple of the players, and they seem with it. So you go for it.

But what if all their players will be arrayed in somber blue and grey pinstripe suits with white shirts and common red ties? Their ad materials and brochures are traditional? Should you consider doing something a bit different anyway? Yes. The goal in the oral is to distinguish your firm from the competition.

Do you have enough courage to prepare a fresh and original oral presentation? Probably. If you are in a creative field — marketing, public relations, advertising, space design — it will be easier, because originality is your business. Firms in public accounting, architecture, or engineering need more resolve to make the change. They must want to stand out from the other teams of presenters.

If you are still resisting the idea of breaking the mold, recognize what it's like when you're the buyer, sitting in a room all day listening to team after team present their credentials. At the end you have masses of notes, a stack of heavy notebooks, and piles of glossy, expensive-looking brochures, and a massive headache. Exhausted, you exclaim, *"I like the group with the big red sombreros. I can't remember what they said, I just remember liking them.* What happened? They did something creative that planted themselves in your memory. Like a great story, a red sombrero reiterated a theme or made a point that caused you to remember.

Take-away Sentence:

Seize the opportunity provided
to demonstrate special qualities
that can be shown only orally.

REASON 11

"We don't need visuals."

The Problem:

Talking heads have very little chance of connecting with an audience. The presenter who attempts to win an audience to her point without visuals must be a superb speaker with a compelling message and spellbinding delivery. Most of us are not spellbinders.

The Solution:

Decide what kinds of visual aids are appropriate for your particular audience, learn to create them (or have them created) and learn to use them well.

Why Visuals?

Visuals are vital for success in the public speaking world today for two key reasons, both related to technology. First, an increasing number of members of your audiences have grown up with television. They demand, color, flash, and glitter. Television viewers are used to being pitched with high profile excitement. Few visual aids can replicate television (although videotaped segments attempt to, if an unlimited budget is available).

Visuals are important because they highlight, supplement, and add dimension to the connection you create with the audience. The attention span of the video generation is much shorter than for those of us who grew up prior to multimedia. This generation is used to constant change, constant color, constant motion, constant excitement and dynamism; your talking head can be weak indeed.

Are we presumptuous to even try keeping the attention of the multimedia generation? Perhaps. Yet visuals, carefully conceived and powerfully presented, will help bridge the gap between the talking head and the multimedia generations.

Second, visual aids are necessary today because, since technology has made it easy to create them, audiences expect them. Computer programs which create graphics abound; many programs draw and paint; giant typefaces, fancy fonts, and attractive borders are all available at the press of a key. Entrepreneurs have set up shops whose sole purpose is turning your rough sketch into a drawing, an elegant layout, or a great word slide. In fact, you are looked upon as lazy or at least out of touch with the rest of the world if you don't have visuals. Your audience is apt to wonder where you have been the last decade.

Are there times when no visual aids should be used? Yes:

- when they are second rate, and your product is first rate
- when you're being honored
- when they're just laundry lists of phrases
- when you don't know how to let them aid you.

Poor Quality Visuals. If second-rate visuals will adversely affect your image, avoid them. Visuals reflect you in the same way that your appearance does (in fact, in the same way that your professional brochures and business cards do).

Don't use visuals unless they are as high in quality as your work, service, or cause. Instead develop and use the support of your voice and your body to their fullest.

Inappropriate Times for Visuals. In general visuals are not appropriate when you receive praise, an award or other recognition. Don't use any aids when giving a commencement address or receiving an honorary degree.

Shun Laundry Lists of Ideas. You shouldn't use visuals if they are just laundry lists of bulleted sentences or long phrases. You shouldn't use visuals if your entire speech is on those visuals and all you're doing is providing transition words and phrases. Your transition words are primarily housekeeping words, such as *the next slide shows...*, *this graph represents..., Next, I'd like to tell you about....*

When You Don't Know How To Use Them. Finally, you don't need visuals if you're just going to read them. Learn to let them help you.

Great visual aids turn a good presentation into an outstanding one. They're called visual **aids** for a very good reason; they aid or support you. **You're** the star, not the visual. The primary rule when you're using a visual is *Use it or lose it.* If a visual is directly amplifying, illustrating, expanding what you're saying, have it on the screen and refer to it. If you're not referring to it, make it go away. Turn it off, cover it up, advance to a black slide if you're using slides. The screen is a huge source of light; a visual up there it attracts a good deal of attention, and you don't want it competing with you.

What Visuals?

You are familiar with graphics used in your profession. Certain kinds of information — and thus certain professions — lend themselves to specific types of graphics and other visuals. When preparing to speak to a group other than your peers, read appropriate professional magazines to find kinds of visuals your audience relates to best. As with your content, visuals should evolve from the perspective of the audience, not from your perspective.

Effective visual aids capture many words in a single picture, a found object, diagram, or phrase. Clarity and simplicity are the rule. Turn concepts into evocative pictures, numbers into dramatic graphs, complex systems into simple flow charts. Look around your workplace for effective props: scientists have intriguing apparatus; architects have cunning scale models; foresters have tiny seedlings; lawyers have imposing books of law; government officials have weighty tomes of code. Every profession has a variety of colorful posters which can be used with success. Hold up a copy of your company newsletter as you read a quote from the president.

Just because an item is commonplace to you, do not overlook its potential as an exciting or meaningful visual for an audience. "Found objects," or props, which represent some significant aspect of your business can heighten interest.

A chiropractor speaking to a civic group brought a most dramatic visual. She strode up to the front of the room carrying a three-foot curved object composed of segments and uneven edges. She began her presentation with a question in a compelling voice, *How many of you have one of these?* Few hands were raised. *You all do.... It's a spine,* she laughed. And we all laughed. She walked silently around the room allowing us to touch it, run our fingers over the nerve nodules and get "up close and personal" with an object that we are all familiar with in another context. She had a dramatic opener, a wonderful visual aid, and a successful presentation.

Here are four basic categories for visuals based on the material they represent: numbers, systems, physical items, and people. In business, most visuals are apt to be related to numbers. In engineering and the sciences, visuals tend to be drawings and diagrams that show physical items. Computer scientists rely on flow charts. Social scientists and government workers rely on graphs bar and pie charts, and pictograms. Finance relies heavily on charts and graphs. Construction and manufacturing graphics, especially for safety concerns, are often people drawings.

Keep It Simple. It's logical that detail-oriented professionals in engineering, software development, or science wish to include all the details, just as financial types want to include the complete "picture" with all the numbers. You do so at your peril. The audience needs simple uncluttered visuals to observe and learn from. Prepare only what the **audience** needs and can understand, not what you would like to offer.

Graphics for Numbers, Statistics, and Financial Data

Graphics for financial data **must** speak for themselves. If you have to interpret them for the audience, they're too complex. Your goal is to translate numbers — dollars, percents, degrees, or demographics — into pictures, for

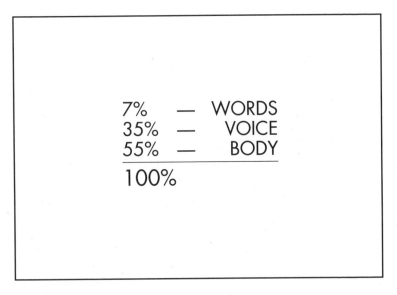

Poor Visual

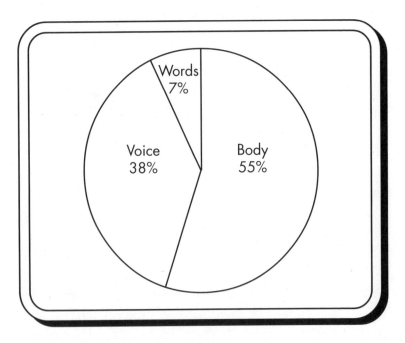

Improved Version

clarity, simplicity, and emphasis. Appropriate graphic devices include bar charts, pie charts, graphs, and pictographs (see opposite page). Be aware that popular newspapers and business magazines have gone too far with cute pictographs overlays, and clever frames for bar charts and pie charts. Too far, that is, for a business presentation.

Avoid tables and any other full pages of numbers, such as balance sheets or profit and loss statements. A full page of numbers is just as bad as a full page of sentences. Though the use of full pages of numbers is common, they are not acceptable as visual aids, for three key reasons:

- number slides can't be absorbed. They have to be read, just like word slides
- the numbers are too small to be read beyond the third row
- they contain extraneous information.

One client asked for advice on speech delivery but not advice about visuals. During the video-taping of the dry run, he presented a bad case of "ineffective table-itis." The speaker was a noted management consultant; his audience, a group of accountants. The first full-page table appeared, accompanied by these words, *I know you can't see the numbers in this table. I wish you could because the numbers tell the story.* Groan. When a speaker says he knows the audience can't see the tables, their reaction has to be *If he knows we can't see them, why is he using them?*

Tables and income statements are also too complex; by nature they contain data that is irrelevant to the point the visual is amplifying. They also can't be read beyond the third row.

Graphs with more than three lines of data are too complex unless you use an overlay. One of my sophisticated financial clients used to get by with transparencies made directly from pages from their proposal (below). Easy, but almost totally unsuccessful, for those same three reasons: the graphs depicted a more complex story than the speaker

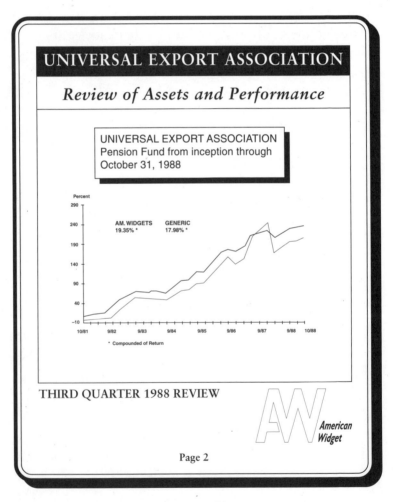

Poor Graphic

wanted to convey; the numbers were too tiny to be read by most of the audience; the visuals were busy.

Don't copy a page from your written report onto a transparency or slide. The transparency will show not only the table or graph, but also the firm name, the client name, the name of the proposal, the framework around the chart and the page number of the report. If you're going to re-produce a report page, simplify it. Physically cut out just the chart or graph, enlarge it on the copier and then create your transparency. The extraneous matter will be gone, the graphic can be read (See below and opposite page).

Remind yourself that the audience doesn't want or need the depth of complexity you routinely use. For financial data, translate the significant data into a simple chart or graph which speaks for itself.

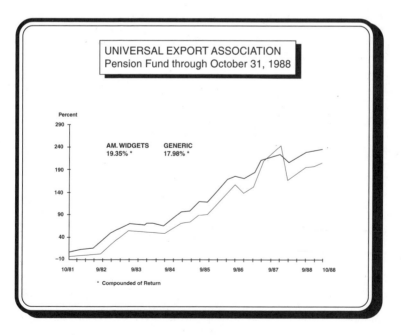

Improved Version

Graphics for Systems, Organization, Flow, and Time Lines

The goal is to show systematic development, relationships, steps in a process, order of events, or to simplify systems and concepts. It takes many words to describe what is simple to illustrate visually. Imagine how many words it would take to explain the typical organizational chart: what the layers of management are, which divisions report to which senior managers, which departments come under which division. Your choices in this category include organizational charts, flow charts, Warnier-Orr diagrams and Gantt charts.

Beware of deciding on an organizational chart, though, because they usually signal that you're talking about yourselves instead of about the audience. The test for such a visual is that you can tie in the explanation to how that organizational structure benefits the audience.

All types of flow charts can simplify your explanation of a process. Know what point you are supporting, and resist the impulse to include every nuance of the process. Remember that the audience doesn't want to know everything you know. Label just the key sections, disclose it gradually, or use the overlay technique (See below).

Graphics for Physical Items

Graphics for physical items are designed to show the relationship of parts to a whole, to illustrate physical systems, to clarify intricate design and development, to show physical connections, to demonstrate complexity. Professions which use such aids would not function day to day without them. Yet too few speakers from these professions take the extra time needed to create speech visuals which could give greater life and vigor to their presentations. Graphics in this category include drawings, exploded drawings, cutaway drawings, renderings, photographs, diagrams, and maps. Software is especially helpful to speed the task of creating such visuals.

When reproducing a depiction of a physical item for a visual, limit the amount of information that you plan to show. To improve these complicated visuals, don't make the reproduction complex and don't label all the parts or fields.

A software company preparing for a national two-day marketing and training seminar asked my advice for polishing their presenters. As one speaker after another was unable to stay even close to the her allotted time, it became evident that one problem rested primarily in their visuals. Because each diagram contained too much detail, the speakers found themselves explaining every one of those details, rather than just those they had prepared to cover. After we whited out some of the detail on the overheads, the speakers returned to their prepared notes and finished on time.

Visuals for People

People graphics are especially useful in creating safety reminders, physical training and new production procedures. Cartoons, sketches and line drawings are common ways to depict people, and they are easy to create with graphics packages such as Corel Draw and Adobe Illustrator. Use exaggeration and humor.

Visuals With Words

Words are not "visual." Create word visuals only as a last resort. Challenge yourself or your computer staff to turn words into more interesting graphics.

Using Visuals Correctly

Learn to use those appropriate visuals correctly.

Debriefing the Visual. An excellent visual needs no further explanation. You talk about it only to reinforce the message. Create a single sentence which introduces the visual just before it comes up or just as it comes up, to title it, to set a frame of reference, or to break the news. The news is whatever the visual is doing as support: it's expanding, it's elaborating, it's demonstrating, it's reflecting... This one sentence gives the significance of the visual. Immediately demonstrate what point it is making. Then pause, giving the audience time to absorb what you've said and look at the rest of the visual. **Do not talk while they are absorbing the visual.** If you continue to use the visual, demonstrate with your hand, as well as with your voice, what is important about it.

Make the visual disappear when you are finished with it or not referring specifically to it. Eliminating the light source is important because the huge white light will detract from you and what you have to say. To eliminate the light source for transparencies, turn it off. With slides, place a black slide between each colored slide so when you click the remote control the screen is empty.

Your Position at the Screen. When using a visual, stand at the screen to encourage eye contact where you

point. The more complicated the visual is the more important it is that you direct their eyes. While they are looking,
observing, and thinking, be quiet.

Let the visual speak, and then get rid of it. The rule is
"Use it or lose it," so it's not competing with you.

Be at the screen to use your visual, not at the projector,
for these reasons:

- You don't want the attention of the audience to be
  divided between you and the screen.
- You are reminded to use the visual.

Auditioning to coach a client's client for a specific
project, I was asked to videotape and critique a senior
member of the firm. He presented fifteen minutes of a media session that he had given the previous day. With slide
projector remote control firmly in hand he proceeded to
speak, flashing up slide after slide — with never a specific
reference or comment to the content of the slide itself. I
first asked, *What were the slides for?* Recognition gradually dawned on this man that not only had he failed to use
the slides appropriately, he had competed with them at every moment of the presentation.

Use your hand (palm out, fingers extended) to point to
the spot on the screen where you want the audience to
look, whether it's the heading, a part of the diagram, totals
near the bottom. You control the audience's eye contact
with the visual. Don't use a pencil, pen, or telescoping
pointer because they turn out to be playthings — to jiggle,
click, or telescope in and out — without your realizing it.
You're less apt to make a plaything of your hand. If you
use a pointer, train yourself to lay it down each time you
finish pointing. If that's difficult to remember, learn to do
it right: use your hand.

If the room is huge and the screen is too far away for you to walk back and forth, acquire a laser pointer. A laser pointer adds sophistication, but only if you practice enough that you use it smoothly. Otherwise, the bouncing red dot looks like a singalong without the words. Don't play with it.

When the distance between projector and screen allows easy movement with overhead transparencies, disclose the material gradually by using overlays or a half sheet of paper as a cover. Add an overlay or pull the paper down as you talk about the exposed information. Those with expensive graphics packages can disclose by creating building visuals, overheads or slides in which one new item of information is added to each succeeding slide. This approach achieves the same effect as disclosing. The greatest disadvantage, aside from cost, is the number of slides you are required to have. See the next chapter for a further discussion.

No Eye Contact, No Voice. Be sure to talk to your audience, not to the visual. We've all been in audiences where the speaker spent most of her time with her back to us, talking to the screen. The rule of thumb is "No eye contact, no voice." Do the adjusting and the walking that you need to do silently. Look at the visual to get your perspective, place your hand where you want it, turn around toward the audience, and only then begin speaking. The audience is patient. They will wait for you. They do not expect you to be talking every moment. In fact, the pauses help them gather their thoughts, process their reactions, and prepare for the next point. Pauses are your friend. Do not be afraid of silence.

Another Don't: Repeating the Handouts

Presenting at a conference, it's important to have hand-outs, because the audience wants the details to take home. You want them to have your name, firm name and tele-phone number too. Too many speakers just repeat what's on the handouts. The typical approach is to create the handouts, then simply copy them onto an overhead or a slide. These are often laundry lists of point after point about point after point, often bulleted, which is good. But they're usually full sentences rather than words or brief phrases.

Your visual should support your dialogue, not contain it. If you announce that three factors have led to the de-cline in value of the dollar, a slide simultaneously flashing on the screen with those three points, you're being redun-dant. Too often the handouts and the visuals present the entire speech. All the speaker does is provide the transition phrases to move from one overhead to the next. Boring. If you're one of those presenters, do something fresh.

Don't Read. People don't like to be read to. If you are primarily a reader, you might as well just send the packet of handouts, and save the meeting. The time with an audi-ence face to face is special time. Use it to connect with the audience; if you can, they'll read the details on the hand-outs afterwards.

Take-away Sentence:

Appropriate visual aids, appropriately used, can make you a star.

REASON 12

"You bet we have visuals... the fanciest visuals electronics can create."

The Problem:
  Today's software can create visuals that become the star. The speaker merely narrates a slide show.

The Solution:
  Keep control of the electronics so that they work for you. Create exciting graphics that support you, not overwhelm you.

What's the Matter With Fancy Visuals?

Isn't it ironic that the best thing that's happened to visual support and the worst thing that's happened to visual support are the same? It's easy to create fancy slides or overheads.

Some users think these programs are technically impressive; lots of people are impressed by technology. Others think they're wonderful because the slides can be in vivid colors and the words can be big enough to be read from the last row of the audience. Drawings and other mechanical data are relatively easy to create. Financial speakers can develop four or five varieties of charts that show the same information in different ways: pie charts, graphs, pictograms, bar charts. The speaker can illuminate the numbers, statistics, and percentages. These fancy visual aids are popular because you can generate them yourself — with changes until the last minute.

You can also change them if your speech coach says you have too many slides that are too fancy, too colorful, too varied, too busy — the downside of these exciting programs.

Once mastered, creating visuals with these programs are easy — too easy. The typical slide or overhead created through one of these packages typically has two problems: too much color and too much busyness.

Color Problems. The wide range of color choices is seductive; it's too easy to select many different colors and shadings, distracting from the message. The popular fades and tones can't be distinguished and do not project well in a large or poorly lit room. These too-colorful visuals can give the impression of a circus poster.

Busyness Problems. Graphics programs offer too many patterns, too many elaborate borders and highlight devices. It's too easy to generate word slides with too many different typefaces, diagrams that are too complex or drawings with too much detail.

Why so many problems? The technology has a way of taking over the process. The programs work too well; most people don't control them. The thinking is, if a little color is good, a lot of color is great. If a little border or shading around the edges is good, a lot of shading with several different colors and a fancy border is even better. And because it's easy to type lots of words, there are lots of words.

Everyone who uses a graphic package has to learn to be the master of the process. One client said with great [misdirected] pride, *Our graphics are so good we look like the Monday Night Football half time show.* Unfortunately for him, that's not the objective. If your graphics look as good as the Monday Night Football half time show, why have a speaker? Why not just make a videotape and send it?

Why the speaker, indeed? **Because the speaker is the star.** The speaker is there to make a connection. No matter how wonderful the visual is, it cannot make the connection one human can make to other humans. It can't create the chemistry. It can't answer questions or start a dialogue.

So, use this wonderful software, but control its use. Visual aids are supposed to do exactly what they say: aid you in the successful presentation of your message. Visual aids support your verbal efforts; they do not replace your words and they should not overwhelm your words. The speaker who hides behind a session which flashes 60 slides in 60 minutes at an unsuspecting audience has not yet learned this basic lesson.

Remember a grand Broadway play *The Little Shop of Horrors*, starring a plant that grows and grows, gradually taking over the entire shop? That's precisely what happens with fancy visuals: they take over the entire process. The resulting visual aids become the visual star. The speaker is in the shadows. An average speaker will find it impossible to dominate such state-of-the-art visuals. Mere mortals become inadequate by comparison.

Keep visuals as aids. Follow simple guidelines for creating visuals that know their place.

Guidelines for Better Visuals

1. Aim for cleanness and clarity. Resist the impulse to be too fancy; even though your computer system enables you to mix six different typefaces, don't. Don't let the art overwhelm the message (See opposite page).

2. Aim for simplicity. To test content, ask a 13 year old to look at your visual and tell you what it says. When using a drawing of a mechanism, resist the temptation to fill in or label all the fields or parts. Include enough detail for authenticity. Label those parts necessary to make the point that that specific graphic is supporting, plus one or two major items for perspective.

3. When developing word visuals, be brief. Use words or short phrases, not sentences. Use single-syllable words whenever possible. Use common abbreviations (you can explain them as you debrief the slide, see page 114).

4. Use capital and lower case lettering rather than all caps. People read more quickly by scanning the ascenders and descenders (the parts of letters which come above and below the regular line of type). Use bold when you want extra emphasis, instead of capital letters.

5. Use color. Remember your multimedia audiences; but resist the opportunity to be gaudy. One or two colors delineating levels of details, plus a accent color for bullets is ample. More than three is too many.

6. Headings or titles should be in the largest type. Subheads should be in the same font (type style), but with slightly smaller type. Consider bold, highlighting or some other special treatment for emphasis of a key word or phrase.

7. For bold visual impact on short lists, use bullets, closed boxes, or closed circles rather than asterisks or open characters.

8. If you have more than three items in a subhead, consider numbering or lettering them. If the items must be taken in order — they are steps in a process,

Poor Visual

The Essence of Communication

- To inform

- To educate

- To convince, persuade, or build good-will

- To get action

Improved Version

for example — numbering them is essential; number-ing reminds the audience of the importance of keep-ing them in order.

THE PURPOSES OF
COMMUNICATING IN BUSINESS

1. To communicate MEANINGFUL and USEFUL ideas or information to a (usually) specific audience.

2. To build goodwill.

3. To get action.

Every word that is used in a business communication — telephone call, interview, memo, letter — must meet one (or more) of these purposes. Otherwise time is be-ing wasted for both the sender and the receiver.

Poor Visual

PURPOSES

• Communicate ideas or information

• Build goodwill

• Get action

Improved Version

NOTE — if the material requires more depth than subheads, print that extra material only on the paper copy of the handouts (and tell them that the detail is there.) Any word overhead or slide should have only the title and the briefly phrased, bulleted subheads.

What Signals Do You Send With Fancy Visuals?

Recently I helped prepare presenters from a large organization who were the speakers for the company's annual international sales meeting. Their audiences would consist of outside sales reps, independent contractors who had this company's product as one of their product lines. Two bright young presenters had acquired the requisite software and had learned it. They had also purchased equipment that used a laptop computer and an overhead to project directly on the screen from the computer disk. They went wild. Their visuals were like Joseph's legendary Coat of Many Colors, with the addition of many words and many bullets. Their visuals overwhelmed them. Like kids with a new toy they had let the technology control their process.

Not only that: because it was so easy, they also created building slides, adding tens of extra slides to their already crammed presentation. (A building slide adds the next point from a laundry list to each succeeding slide. With a six bullet laundry list you end up with seven slides. Instead of having three basic slides, one for each main point, you can easily have 20 or more.) Consider that a typical business speaker creates about 20 slides for his one-hour presentation. With building slides, that number skyrockets to 70 or 80. This isn't even a narrated slide show, because there isn't time to inject words; it's simply button pushing.

Too many slides with many words on every slide sends a distinct message about your lack of competence — and confidence — as a speaker. You are saying, just as clearly as you can, *I don't think I can say these words in such a way that they'll be meaningful to you, so I'm going to write them up so you can read them.*

Emphasizing a Point

Some people try defending their over-many over-wordy slides this way: *I write this up just like I said it to empha-size the point.* But mere repetition is not the most satisfactory way to emphasize. Better to emphasize with your voice and gestures. Here are six basic ways to emphasize an idea (interestingly, none of these use a visual):

1. Say the word. Say it's *important, key, vital, significant, primary.*
2. Number it. *There are two concerns here. First...second....*
3. Use your voice. Say it louder, say it slower.
4. Use a gesture to support it.
5. Pause. Pause before it, pause especially after it.
6. Repeat it. Say it again with a little more emphasis or a little more enthusiasm.

Some ideas in a speech are so important you should employ all six of these devices. What does that leave for visuals? Concepts, pictures, diagrams — which, to quote an old saying, are worth a thousand words.

Take-away Sentence:

*Drive the technology,
don't let it drive you.*

REASON 13

"I have enthusiasm. That's the key thing."
Or
"I'm too nervous to let my enthusiasm show."

The Problem:
Unbounded enthusiasm is often served up alone. Without a coherent message, the speaker's enthusiasm leaves the audience excited but empty. Without a means to tap that enthusiasm, the audience leaves excited but frustrated.

The Solution:
Enthusiasm is crucial. But it can't get the job done alone. Get an audience excited with your delivery and give them a message to take away — and use.

Why Isn't Enthusiasm Enough?

Here are some stories to illustrate the need for at least one of these two additions to enthusiasm: a take-away message and a call to action.

Enthusiasm Without Control. One of my clients has so much enthusiasm that he practically has to be restrained with ropes. He is so committed to his product and such an energetic, exciting person that he almost explodes when he talks. The rest of the staff lives in fear that one day he will spontaneously combust on stage. He is extremely knowledgeable about his products and his industry niche. With abundant knowledge and natural comfort in front of an audience, he assumes he can just wing it. But the result is lots of content, not organized; and lots of enthusiasm, not channeled. Audiences get an abundance of knowledge, but it isn't focused to give them anything to take away to use. Excitement is developed, but they have no place to go with their excitement; it is not pointed to any particular purpose.

He has developed into a great storyteller, too, and can retell stories beautifully. But in the telling, the tales become longer and longer, funnier and funnier. Soon he becomes an entertainer, not a speaker — and not a seller with a message about his product.

My task was to help him maintain the enthusiasm, but use it as one of his tools rather than the major element in his presentation style. That change required his having a clearer purpose for each presentation, a focused single sentence he was moving the audience toward. It also required his developing particular stories to use in particular situations, rather than falling back on every story that he knew. And he can: public speaking is a skill and he's mastering it.

Enthusiasm Without Content. Another example of enthusiasm that has insufficient focus is projected by the typical motivational speaker. Everyone has heard great motivational speakers with wonderful intonation, dynamic pauses, heartfelt tone of voice. These speakers send audiences away feeling inspired, very up and excited — but often the audience has nothing to take away to use later. People express great excitement about an inspirational speaker: *Oh, he's wonderful! He's just great, just an inspiring speaker.* My typical response is, *Great. What did you learn? What did you take away? What can you use in your own life?* The reply is, *Oh, hmm, he's just a great speaker.* And I persist, *I understand he's a great speaker. What was his message? What did he give you, besides inspiration?* Their response is, *Oh, I can't really tell you. I don't know.* In other words, there wasn't a take-away message.

Failing to Relate Material to the Audience. What about speakers who have enthusiasm and interesting material but don't relate it to the needs of the audience? A colleague of mine is a government official who frequently attends conferences, hearing a variety of speakers. He remembers hearing one nationally known speaker who came to motivate. Her speech was filled with pithy one-liners, and lots of quotable material. Also a sophisticated speaker, he said he felt distanced from the material. It wasn't related to him or his work. He told me he found himself sitting back with his arms folded, saying, *So?*

If your audience is saying *So?*, you have not connected your material to them. You may reach your audience because of your enthusiasm, but not connect with them by not relating your message to their needs.

So much for inspiration without a take-away message. Former NFL referee Jim Tunney captured the essence of motivation. He said that motivation is a like a bath: it doesn't last long, so you need one every day.

Creating Enthusiasm Without an Outlet

Another problem with speakers who rely on great enthusiasm is that a speech rousing people to a fever pitch ultimately fails unless there is an outlet provided for that pent-up emotion. If you're going to tap into people's emotions and rouse them to action, give them some focus for it! In my city one hears stories of a prominent civic leader who gives rousing speeches with a dynamic voice, great gestures, and tremendous enthusiasm. But too often he fails to channel the energy he creates by giving concrete suggestions for specific action. (In sale circles we say he fails to ask for the sale.) After one such rousing speech, I heard a listener say, *Wow! All that energy he brought to the surface. Couldn't you just feel the excitement in the room? He needed to offer a plan to tap it or channel it. But there was no call to action. What a waste!*

Enthusiastic speakers tend to violate Marian's key rule for speaking: *It's not what you want to say that matters, it's what the audience needs to hear.* If you have great speech skills, especially tremendous enthusiasm, you have a responsibility to provide an outlet for the energy that you generate in the audience. Be sure your message is related to the needs of the audience and includes a take-away idea.

Speaking With No Enthusiasm

And if you have the opposite problem? You don't have enough enthusiasm or you're not able to project the enthusiasm that you feel because of nervousness, anxiety, or outright fear? Your problem is primarily one of attitude adjustment. Henry Ford once said, *Whether you think you can or cannot, you're always right.* He was certainly talking about speakers. You're your own worst enemy when fear is the problem. Most people can channel their nervousness; many can eliminate it.

Having enthusiasm as a speaker is crucial: No one in the audience is going to be more fervent than the speaker. Enthusiasm is one quality that comes naturally to many people because they are excited about their product, their services or their topic. Clients sometimes report that one-to-one they have no trouble being enthusiastic; it's just when they get in front of a group they become wooden.

If you can do it for one, you can do it for one hundred. Projecting enthusiasm is a skill, and it can be developed. In the same way that musicians and athletes get better, by learning new skills and practicing them, speakers can get better.

Enthusiasm is a combination of a lively, interesting voice and natural, logical gestures which support that voice. The key to enthusiasm, of course, is that you really do mean what you say. You have a commitment to the concept, product, or service. Developing your voice and gestures comes from that genuine commitment. The stumbling block, of course, is fear.

When a prospective client says to me, *Marian, I'm a terrible speaker,* my response is usually, *I'll bet you are.* Here's why I'm so direct with such confidence: people who are fearful of speaking have thought about that fear and expressed it so many hundreds, even thousands, of times, it becomes a huge self-fulfilling prophecy.

Two steps will speed you toward your goal of more enthusiastic public speaking. Develop an attitude which says **I can**; concentrate on a mind set that lets **I can** be true. Then develop and practice warm-ups that channel the natural tension to work **for** you, not against you.

Developing the I Can *Attitude.*

The first step is to develop an *I can* attitude, using self talk, visualizing, or affirmations. Self-talk includes reminders to yourself that this presentation is important, it's going to go well, you are prepared, you are confident. Positive self-talk replaces — banishes — the negative things you used to say.

Affirmations work well for many people. A variation of self-talk, in an affirmation you create positive statements of worth or success which focus on the desired result. Speech affirmations could include such affirming statements as *I am a good speaker and I am getting better,* or *Speaking comes naturally to me.* Repeat an affirmation until you believe it. Then it will be so.

A third approach for success is visualizing. Visualizing involves mentally accomplishing an activity in advance of actually accomplishing it. For an upcoming speech, visualizing means enacting the presentation in your mind prior to giving it. Create a mental home movie or videotape of yourself successfully giving the presentation. Put yourself in a quiet room where there are no distractions and create a film of yourself — see yourself seated at the head table; visualize yourself walking confidently to the lectern, establishing eye contact, delivering your dramatic first sentence, developing your thesis, presenting your oral guidelines, gesturing freely and comfortably. See the finish with your strong close. Visualize the applause that will come when you're finished.

Visualizing yourself succeeding increases your confidence. Visualizing also gives you an opportunity to see which parts of the process you are most comfortable about and which parts need more work. I find that certain parts seem harder to visualize; those are the parts which need more attention. If I can go smoothly through the entire presentation in the visualization process, then I am confident I am prepared. But if I find myself pausing hesitantly in visualizing one part of the process, that's a signal that an area needs more preparation or practice.

A final tip for pre-speech attitude adjustment is what athletes call "putting on your game face." In other words, getting yourself revved up. In the locker room before the game someone often gives a little pep talk, *Let's go get 'em! Everybody step up! This is for all the marbles!* Players have their own mental warm-up routines. One of the most unusual routines may be that of Atlanta Braves rightfielder. According to his wife, Halle Berry: *Driving to the stadium I have to start a fight with him because he plays better if he's a little agitated.* Imagine what would happen if a baseball player did not think about the game at all, but simply went out and tried to swing his bat. Unless a player thinks about what he is going to do, thinks about his role in the game and his ability to contribute to the team effort, he won't be ready. Putting on your game face is exactly that, getting ready. You need the same approach. It's specific revving-up words in a revved-up tone to get in high gear before the presentation. You must begin your presentation in high gear. The audience is not likely to be patient while you get warmed up.

Putting on your game face involves getting the right mental attitude just before you speak. Work on enthusiasm while driving or in your hotel room. Go into the rest room, make sure your hair is controlled and your tie straight, and rev up your enthusiasm.

Dorothy Sarnoff, a well-known former speech trainer, describes her approach to attitude adjustment. She suggests motivating phrases to help speakers be ready for the moment. Say to yourself, *I'm glad I'm here. I'm glad you're here. I care about you. I know that I know.*

Examine these four statements for a minute. *I'm glad I'm here* gives you permission to express your real enthusiasm, assuming that you have it.

I'm glad you're here acknowledges you remember that the speech is for the audience and not for you.

I care about you reinforces demonstrating that care by giving them what they need and want, not just what you want to say.

I know that I know is the final confidence builder. You say to yourself, as I've indicated, *I'm the expert here. I'm the one they came to listen to. They want what I have to say. They're interested in this message. I know that I can give them what they want.*

Many speakers may still feel some nervousness. Plan a gesture or activity early in the speech to combat final nerves. Johnny Carson, long time host of the *Tonight* show, reportedly had a heartbeat of 180 beats a minute prior to beginning. His big golf swing before the monologue acted as that last tension reliever.

Others are still nervous because they waited too long to begin preparing their minds. Preparing your mind begins when you first get the assignment or decide to speak. Speaking is a part of your professional duty; preparing your mind to speak is part of that work.

Warm-ups — It's Hard To Be Tense If You're Flexible

A positive mindset ensures your confidence and the enthusiasm that follows. What about your body? It may still be tense. The solution is pre-speech warm-ups. One secret of warm-ups is **flexibility**. It's hard to be tense if you're flexible. Move your mind to the gridiron, and picture the amount of time football players spend getting their muscles limber and ready. When you run, you stretch leg muscles first. Singers and instrumentalists warm up their voices and their fingers.

Tension is natural. In fact without extra adrenaline you'll be unable to perform well. Learn to use that tension to work for you; channel it by warming up. The warm-up list I give my clients includes warm-ups for face, eyes, mouth, hands, arms, body, voice, and breathe.

Face. Hundreds of tight muscles in your face prevent your natural smile from appearing spontaneously, showing energy and enthusiasm you want to project. Loosen those muscles by making faces. Squint and then fully open your eyes, stretch the skin around your mouth by doing what we called as kids "rubber faces."

Eyes. Eye contact around the room is easier and more comfortable with your eyeballs moving fluidly in their sockets. No, I'm not kidding. Put your index finger out in front of your face about a foot, and move it from side to side. Follow it with your eyes, without moving your head. Or just roll your eyes around for awhile.

Prior to your presentation, you'll be putting your notes and visuals at the table in the front of the room. Stand still and make eye contact with each corner of the room, to remind yourself what range of eye contact you'll need. Then do the same, moving your head and even your body slightly, as you will when speaking.

Mouth. Warm up the many muscles which work your tongue and mouth to create speech with these phrases.

They also provide further warm-up for other facial muscles. Do at least four repetitions of these alliterative sentences:

Bob bats blue ball blindly
do dig down deeply
each elephant enters every elevator
furiously flex your fiddle finger
good guys get great glory
Lorinda lovingly lingers longer
mop messes from my massive mantle
please plump purple pillows proudly
ten tall turtles tumble terrifically
zestfully zap the zebra's zipper.

Hands. Spread your fingers out and create some muscular tension. Now flex them. Make and release a fist several times.

If you're still feeling tense just before it's your turn, do some subtle isometrics by making and releasing fists under the table. Or grip and release the sides of your chairseat a few times. You should be able to feel the tension slipping out of your body.

Arms. Do windmills, push against a wall, or flex your biceps. Limbering up your arms will make it easier for your brain to get the gestures it will be requesting. My favorite arm loosener is one of the many warm-ups basketball players do prior to tip-off: let your arms hang comfortably by your sides, vigorously shaking your hands as if to shake water from them.

Body. Try a few deep knee bends. Stretch your hamstrings as if you were about to go jogging. Do the twist, hands on hips, lower body still, upper body turning from side to side.

The theory with all the warm-ups is that it is difficult to maintain tension in your body if the muscles are loosened and working. Your body will be ready to go to work. Physical warm-ups also keep your mind occupied.

Voice. Vocal cords are key instruments in your presentation. Anyone planning to speak for at least 20 minutes needs to limber up the vocal cords, even if not nervous, to prevent hoarseness from setting in. Even if you can't sing, sing, *La la la la la la la,* each *la* higher and firmer than the last. You can even sing this warm-up silently if you have no privacy. Vocal cords are another area which will perform much better if you warm them up appropriately.

The debilitating cotton mouth and the unnerving early squeak can generally be eliminated with such warm-ups. Avoid milk and cold drinks prior to speaking; shun the ice water pitcher, selecting hot water or tea.

Breathing. The old standby, a few slow deep breaths, can be your final physical warm-up. Of course, if you're hyperventilating, slow, shallow breathing is indicated.

Last, and most fun, play some music that energizes you. Ideally a tape that you can play in your car, this music will be an artist and a song which set your toes tapping, make your body move to the music. My rev-up artist is James Brown, belting out *I Feel Good.* His strong beat and driving rhythm can get me moving even if I'm not feeling good. Your music may be Stravinsky, Pink Floyd, Elvis, or Van Morrison. Find it and use it. The music may be all you need!

Let your nervousness help you to be the kind of speaker that you'd like to be. Channel your nervousness to create enthusiasm. The audience can never have more enthusiasm than you have. The enthusiasm, the excitement, the high energy generated by your speech must come first from you.

Take-away Sentence:

Too much enthusiasm is as bad as too little enthusiasm.

REASON 14

"It's a speech, not a workshop. Why would I want to involve the audience?"

The Problem:
People just won't sit still for lecturing anymore.

The Solution:
Include the audience. Move them from passive listeners to active participants. Involve them mentally, physically, in writing, or orally.

Why Involve the Audience?

As discussed earlier, your approach and your success are based on your ability to get the audience to move from *SO?* or *Who cares?* to *Ohh* or *I can see how that works for me,* or *I'm interested in this.*

You accomplish this goal most easily by moving your audience from listeners to participants through involvement. Once they begin to participate they have a vested interest in your presentation because they are part of it. Remember the Oriental proverb which says: *I hear and I forget. I see and I remember. I do and I understand.*

Video games, interactive computer programs, even the involvement that plain vanilla computing brings to business all cause people to want to participate. They are bored with just listening. Trust me on this, the old way is broken. And as Robert Kriegel reminds us, even if it ain't broke, break it anyway. New ways are needed for new times.

Bill Cosby can get away with just speaking, or lecturing. He uses no visual aids and does not invite the audience to participate. Of course, he's actually not just lecturing. He's telling long hilarious shaggy dog stories, cavorting around the stage, acting out all the parts. Using that wonderfully effective rubber face of his, with 7 voices and 18 different kinds of body movement, Cosby visually recreates what happened in his stories. Cosby does involve the audience with aural and visual effects that helps it fit into his picture. It works for him. You need to involve the audience too. Because you're in business presentations, you'll want more business-like involvement.

What About Your Expertise? My clients will say, *But I'm not doing a workshop. They've hired me to give them the benefit of my expertise.* There are certainly situations where your level of expertise is so much greater than the rest of the audience that they're delighted to sit, rapt and thoughtful, as you expound your positions, beliefs, and opinions. More often, though, it's a more successful session if at least some of the information emerges from the audience rather than from the speaker. As the expert asked to speak on the topic of one of my books I even find that true. Involvement devices are the way to make that happen.

Here's an excellent example of how involvement energized audiences. I was asked to use my communicating expertise to help a group of health care people get better compliance from their patients. What they wanted from me was a speech about dealing effectively with difficult patients. I said no.

They were aghast! *Why not? You have so much to tell us.*

I replied, *Yes, I do, but you've also got a lot to tell.* I convinced them to let me create a workshop format. I did have some concern that the group's reaction would be *Well, we're paying this lady, why isn't she doing the work?* This kind of facilitating does take lots of work, but rather than spend time convincing the audience of that, I began the presentation with this comment : *With my thirty years of experience in communicating I have some wonderful ideas for you, but there's lots more than thirty years experience in this room.* A graduated show of hands for time working in health care led to a total experience figure of over 600 years. They were blown away!

It made immediate sense to them why 600 years of experience could solve the problem.

Following the format I had ready, we divided into groups for lively, interesting focused discussions; mini reports and more discussion followed. I added my particular expertise when appropriate. The audience loved it. From the perspective of the organizers, the rest of the conference was a huge success, due partly to how energized the audience had become in our opening interactive session. Organizers got glowing reports, enthusiastic letters and cards (which warmed my heart even more than giving the speech would have) with expressions of feeling empowered and strong.

As the expert, should I have just lectured, or was this involvement a better approach? There was no contest. And since I could add things I was still able to meet my moral commitment to help people with my skills. Was there theory that I didn't get to express? Of course. Were there wonderful stories that I didn't get to tell? Yes. As a speaker, it's hard to leave those elements out. I love to speak. I believe — and my evaluations reflect — that I'm an outstanding speaker. Yet involvement beats lecturing; it's taken me over fifteen years as a professional speaker to move to this conclusion. But involving and empowering the audience empowers me too.

The Journey Is for the Audience. The audience must be involved if it's **their** journey that you are providing. One of the major goals of your introduction is to involve the audience. Even with a ten-minute breakfast speech, involve the audience. The reaction of one client, who frequently does short breakfast meeting speeches was *Well, I have only ten minutes. I can't afford to take any time to involve the audience.* My response, to him and to you, is that you can't afford not to.

Dare to reach your ultimate goal, to get a specific message across, with fresh and original means. People who are part of the process — truly participants and not just observers or listeners — are more attentive, they remember more, and they are more apt to buy your message.

The degree of involvement you select is determined by time and type of presentation you give. Training sessions and meetings that you facilitate demand the most; formal speeches generally require the least. Most presentations fall between these two extremes.

To begin the decision-making process for degree of audience involvement, consider the needs, attitudes, and beliefs of this particular group based on your assessment of them in the Communications Triangle (See Reason Three). Here are four ways to involve your audience:

- involve their minds
- involve them physically
- involve them in writing
- involve them orally.

To decide what methods of involvement to use, ask yourself some questions:

- Where is the audience on this topic?
- How much insight do they already have?
- How much more do they need to buy into my message?
- How willing are they to deal with the problem-solving we need?
- Do they need to know how I work?
- Will my choice of involvement devices help show them how I work?
- How much involvement is needed to get a commitment from them?

Focus the involving aspect of your introduction on their concerns. In other words, speak to their need, not just from your own.

As a rule of thumb, the further you need to move an audience, the more involvement you need. For instance, if your purpose is to educate an audience, let them help themselves by drawing out what they already know, and add you expertise to it.

If you've decided an audience already knows about the problem, your goal is either to convince or to get action. Get them vested in the solution by involving them in the process.

Involve Their Minds

The quickest and simplest method to involve an audience is to involve their minds; there are several ways. Ask them a question, ask them to remember something, get them to recall someone which is relevant to your topic.

If past memories will help get people's minds in the arena where you'll be working, begin with *Remember the last time you...* or *Remember when we first opened and all our business came from word of mouth? Well....* or bring up some old pains with *Consider the last time you were forced to wait, lying flat on your back, while other patients got the doctor's attention. Wouldn't it have helped if someone had whispered to you, "You're next. Hang on."*

Or *Remember the first dollar you earned in this business? I wonder if you still have it.*

Every presentation, no matter how short, can be more successful if you involve the audience at least mentally.

Involve Them Physically

The second method of involving the audience is to get them to do something physical. You can involve the audience physically by asking them to raise their hands in response to some questions. The simple act of raising their hands relaxes their bodies and makes them more receptive to what you have to say. It also involves their minds. If they're sitting in their own little invisible isolation boxes at the beginning of an early morning keynote address or a Saturday training session, some may not have spoken yet. They're rigid or tense.

Your questions should focus on your concerns about preferences, demographics, background, experience: how many of them are homeowners, how long they have worked in this industry, what their level of education or background is, how many of them own new cars, how many of them come from out of state…. The list is endless. Several purposes are served. Consider that you're an out of town computer-aided software engineering expert (anyone from out of town is an expert!).

You might ask the typical "How Long" series, *How many of you have been using CAD systems for three years or more? one year? How many of you are new to CAD?* You might ask for a show of hands on different types of systems being used. If your private agenda is marketing, you might find out (with subtlety) about decision-makers: *How many of you got to select your own systems?* You get the idea. Get them warmed up and also focused on how they relate to your message.

Another desirable and important outcome of asking people to raise their hands about something: you find out additional information you need about the kind of audience you really have. Even though the meeting planners indicated that the audience would be composed of engineers actively involved in software development, you'll want to check that with a show of hands. And however much you already know about the audience ahead of time, you can always find something else to ask which will involve them and also help to individualize your talk.

The story is told of a speaker who was asked to keynote the meeting of the association for New York City taxi cab drivers. He made some assumptions about their level of education and intelligence which he "forgot" to validate with questions at the beginning of his speech. Unfortunately, the assumptions were far too low. Not only was he unsuccessful in individualizing his talk, he was unable to even complete it: He was booed off the stage.

Finally, and of extreme importance to your success, asking people by show of hands to demonstrate their background, their orientation, or their level of experience helps the audience to understand its own diversity. If your topic is broad, some of your material is apt to be basic, some sophisticated or technical. Those who are technical will wonder why you're boring them with background information. Those who are not sophisticated will worry that they're in the wrong session. However, if you ask about years of experience, the audience will understand there's a big range of background. In other words, you help the audience to understand why you have chosen the material by letting them see what experience, backgrounds, and interests are present.

Be sure to ask a wide enough range of questions that everyone gets to raise a hand at least once. There's a danger if some people are left out.

Involve Them in Writing

A third method of involving the audience is to ask them to write. Have them jot down three points, two aspects, five traits, or four features of something. Ask them to write down their expectations for the seminar or the training session. Ask them to write down the first three words that come to their minds when you mention a key word, such as " service," or "authority." Ask them to recollect something or someone and jot down a thought or two. In other words, involve people by getting them to translate thought into action through writing.

My speech *How To Talk So Others Will Listen* has a natural writing opener: I ask each person to cross out the word *others* and write in the name of one specific person whom they would like to get better attention from. If the audience is women, I often add, *And turn the paper over to continue your list on the back,* to much laughter. My involvement device has guided their attention to the topic of our journey; it also forces them to find a particular frame of reference for the tips we'll be analyzing. The physical work, the writing, and the laughter also serve to loosen them up. And do they ever feel like participants.

If you want to add a touch of formality or some organization to the process, include a worksheet in your handouts so they can write these items down in a structured way. Another option is to put big pieces of butcher paper or newsprint on the wall. Ask people to list ideas, reactions, questions, problems, or concerns, on these sheets of paper around the room. This activity not only involves them in writing, it obviously gets them physically up moving around and talking. The goal in involving the audience is to get them to invest themselves in the importance of your topic; asking them to do something heightens the odds of success.

You may be thinking that this sounds more like workshop activity; my response is, so what? Is your primary goal to stand up in front of people or is it to get your point across? Many speeches would be much more successful if developed and run more like workshops, especially those to staff.

Involve Them Orally

Finally, you can involve people orally. This involvement approach is the very best one, even for speeches, because at bottom most of us would rather talk than listen — especially if we can do so from the safety of a group.

Brainstorming. The best tool for oral involvement is some degree of brainstorming. Many speakers are hesitant to involve the audience with brainstorming because they are fearful that too much stuff will come up that they can't possibly cover. Some say that they really need to plan their presentation ahead of time and they're afraid that the points they want to talk about will not come up. That is, they don't know how to control the result of brainstorming. Two points here: First of all, recognize that the purpose of brainstorming is to get people involved, not necessarily to plan your entire speech. People understand that brainstorming is a device to gather lots of ideas and talk about a few of them. Your approach can be to examine the list, check off three particular aspects to focus on. They happen to be the three items that you are most prepared to talk about or that are the most important.

But what happens, you say to me skeptically, if my three points don't get up there? Make sure they do get up there. Seed the list. As people present ideas, you are scribing; when there's a short pause, you say, *What about X?* and write it up. There's more brainstorming, then you say, *Oh, let's not forget...* and you write up the second thing. You get the picture. The chances are good that at least two of the three you have planned probably did come up. But if they didn't, add them to the list and talk about them. If people notice, they won't care. You're the expert, remember?

When you plan a brainstorming activity, come prepared with your own list, in case the brainstorming does not go well.

There are many reasons to brainstorm: involving people; drawing people out; getting real new information; enlarging your own scope; it's a way of helping the audience focus on the aspects you want to talk about. For all those reasons, brainstorming is an important part of your speaker's tools.

With most audiences, responses will flow better if you follow a two-step process instead of just asking for ideas off the top. Recognize that there is a certain amount of vulnerability to expressing oneself in a group. A typical approach with brainstorming is just to get out a big, blank piece of newsprint and ask for suggestions about whatever the topic is. The audience sits and sits, and you're apt to say, *Oh, come on now, you must have some thoughts about this. This is not a test, come on, you can give me some ideas, don't be shy.*

The two-step process of brainstorming nearly always improves the process. You get better, more complete, and quicker response. The first step is to ask people to either think about or jot down things about the topic. Then ask for the ideas orally, writing them up on a flipchart or whiteboard. Sometimes just having everyone hear the ideas brainstormed accomplishes your purpose, without the second step of recording them.

I once turned a prepared keynote speech situation into a massive involvement session through brainstorming. The day-long theme was customer service. I had a one and one-half hour speech prepared, with lots of tips, wonderful ideas, and amusing stories. As I was waiting to be introduced, I gazed at the audience. The thought occurred that in front of me were a hundred people who had experience working in customer service. The chances were excellent, virtually a hundred percent, that most everything I planned to say could be elicited from them.

Right at that moment I changed the presentation. Because it was a big group, mostly strangers to each other, and because it was Saturday morning, we did the two-step brainstorming. First I asked them to jot down on the back of their agendas two or three concerns they had about customer service in their department or in their company.

We brainstormed these out loud. It was quickly clear to them that the practice of customer service was broader than they had been used to thinking. These were their thoughts: customer service is also the people on the phone; each individual represents part of the image of the company in public; customers need to be served within the company too; the data processing department, for example, has customers in the rest of the company; everybody in the company has a customer who is working in some other part of the company. The brainstorming made this point obvious so I simply summarized it and reinforced it.

My planned theme had been "Customer service is more than just the people in the customer service department." I had prepared a similar list to go over, item by item. The second change was to inscribe these areas of broader customer service on sheets, These were written on big sheets, taped on the wall. During a quick break, people signed up for the topic they wanted to tackle. Each group discussed one area for fifteen or twenty minutes, making a list of what was good and what could be improved. We reassembled and groups reported a few highlights. (I was able to assure the groups that management would gather up the lists and distribute them so the results of all their efforts could be shared by everyone.)

We accomplished the same basic points that I had planned to make. But instead of my making the points, with the audience listening and perhaps writing some of them down, they were able to make the points themselves. They became involved in the process and took ownership of the problem. Many of the tools I had planned to give them were expressed by someone during the reports or written on their sheets. I felt free to add extra thoughts that had not been mentioned.

There were comments I had wanted to make which I did not make. But my real purpose was to raise their awareness about the importance of customer service. Less material got communicated overall, but their awareness was much greater for having elicited and developed the material themselves. Was this a successful keynote speech? You bet it was.

To begin customer service training, I typically ask people to think about one place where they especially like to do business, shop, or have a service done. Next they jot down some specific reasons why they like this place of business. Finally, involving them orally, we brainstorm their lists. Responses typically include these: *they know my name, they smile, it's clean, clerks are knowledgeable, they acknowledge my presence even if they're busy, they treat me like a person, not a number.*

Members of the audience quickly realize they already know what good service means — no one needs to tell them. They are ready for the journey I have planned, to re-discover ways to enliven their interest and enthusiasm for offering others the kind of service they like.

This series of involvement devices accomplishes several objectives: getting their minds in my arena, moving them from listeners to participants, and providing both the frame of reference and the content of the presentation themselves.

Socializing. Unless a speech is formal, a good involve-ment activity is a socializing process. With an audience of strangers socializing is the minimal oral activity, and it's an important one if you will want people to participate later. If you plan to ask them to share their feelings or even alter their beliefs during the course of a speech, socializing them first greatly improves your chances of success. If you are on a tight time schedule, this activity can be accomplished in as little as one minute. Ask them to turn to the persons on their left and right and introduce themselves. This kind of involvement, quick as it is, minimizes the strangeness that people feel. With even minimal contact with someone else, people feel less isolated. Socializing is less necessary when your audience knows one another well but still helpful if it's early in the morning or if they aren't well acquainted. When queried, most of my clients admit they haven't thought about the fact that members of their audience — company managers from three different locations, for instance — aren't well acquainted. Yet these clients will ask these relative strangers to consider problems in company sexual harassment policy. Let them connect first, then ask them to spill their guts.

Small group discussions help raise the audience's awareness that differing opinions exist. Complete that two-, five-, or ten-minute discussion with one of the follow-up options above. Sometimes it is enough just to raise awareness that others have differing ideas, the same problems, or new insights and experiences. Awareness helps them solve problems more comfortably; they are also more likely to be open to your suggestions for change.

Socializing a group prior to serious discussion creates greater openness. Added bonuses of socializing activities are that humorous information may come to light, and people find strangers with whom they have something in common. Bonds are formed that improve the session. A few minutes of conversation, shared information, and laughter create participants eager to get on with a speech that becomes theirs, not just yours.

Control the Audience. When you engage an audience in any oral involvement activity, be certain that you can regain control once the activity is complete. If you question your ability to call the group back to attentiveness, prepare a specific transition sentence which ties together their activity and your next topic. Bang a pen on your water glass until you get their attention, then say, *The widespread nature of these problems helps us all understand why it's essential to create at least a first draft of our policy today.*

Though it's hard to give up that straight lecture role, the results are better. Try it, you'll like it.

Take-away Sentence:

Move your audience from listeners to participants.

Index

A

B

C

D

E

F